NOVELS
(Print and E-Books)

"K" Series
Blood Tax
White Gold Tax (coming 2016)

Six Bulls Series
Six Bulls—The Ohioans
The Carolinian
Avenge
Bride by Mail

Six Bulls Series

SHORT STORIES
(E-BOOKS)

Abraham
Arkansas Storm & Captain Jonathan Buzzard
Beanblossom Creek & Stain
Canyon of Death
Danny Boy & Tennie
Roaring River
Runaway Slave
Smoke
Sourdough Wind Mine
Three Bells & Newtonia

Blood Tax

"K" Series of Novels

Richard Puz

EAST 74TH STREET PRESS*WASHINGTON

This book is a work of fiction. Names, characters, businesses, organizations, places, events and incidents either are the product of the author's imagination or used fictitiously. Any resemblance to actual persons, living or dead, events or locales is entirely coincidental.

Copyright © 2016 by Richard Puz

All rights reserved. No part of this book may be reproduced or transmitted, in any form or by any means, without the express written permission of the author.

Cover and images designed by Julie Puz-Wilson

Library of Congress Control Number: 2016938867
East 74th Street Press*Washington, Lacey, WA
ISBN-10: 069268400X
ISBN-13: 9780692684009

First Edition

Dedicated to the love of my life ~

I express my deepest gratitude to family and friends who saw me through the completion of this novel. Without such support, life would indeed be incomplete.

This story draws on many references shown in the bibliography. In particular, the author gratefully acknowledges the work of Dr. Stanislav Južnič, Ph.D., entitled <u>The History of Kostel (1500-1900), Between Two Civilizations</u>, originally published as a Doctoral Thesis in Ljubljana, Slovenia, in 1999; and the subsequent American publication in 2004 by The Slovenian Genealogy Society International, Inc. Without Dr. Južnič's efforts, the small fiefdom of Kostel might have slipped into history without notice. His work was invaluable in writing this novel.

OTTOMAN EMPIRE SIXTEENTH CENTURY

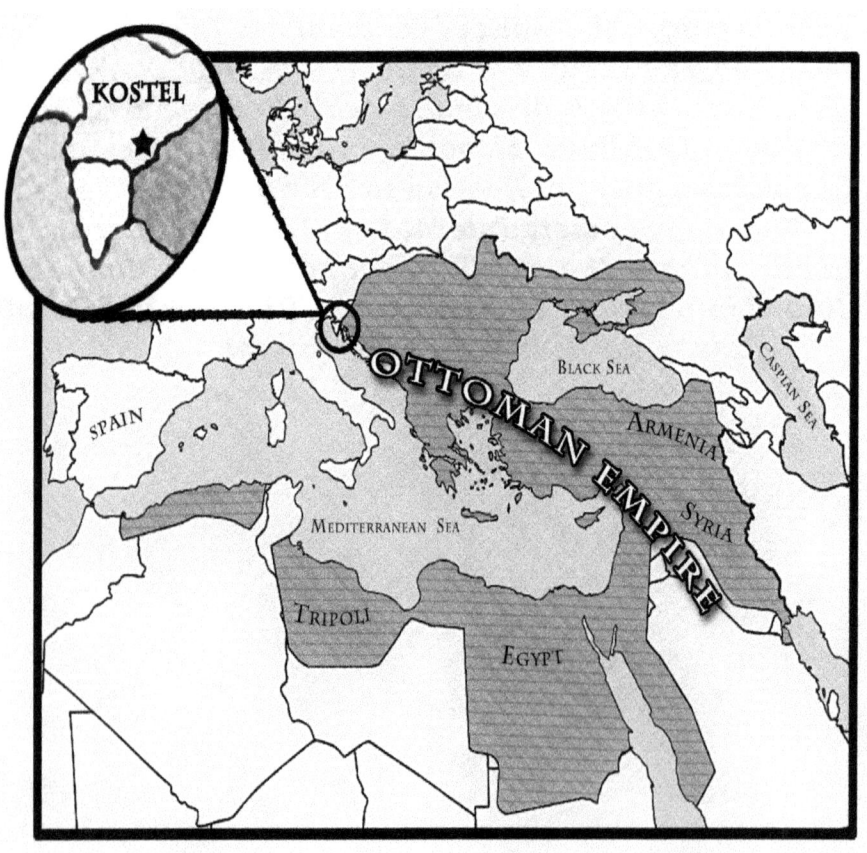

FOREWORD

With the fall of the Roman and the Byzantine empires, the Balkan Peninsula divided between Christian followers under the Hapsburg Monarchy (and later the Austrian Empire and the Austro-Hungarian Empire), and Muslim supporters of the Ottoman Empire. Each was the most powerful adversary of the other during the sixteenth to eighteenth centuries, leading them and their surrogates to fight countless wars, battles and skirmishes.

Turkish soldiers and irregular bandits led frequent attacks on Christian areas of the Balkans for centuries during the Middle Ages, abducting serfs as white slaves while also looting, raping and spreading fear and unrest. The viciousness and frequency of such raids in some parts led people to flee, leaving large tracts of land unoccupied for a century or more.

There was no doubt in the minds of Christian leaders that the Ottoman Empire wished to conquer Vienna and the Hapsburg Monarchy, and the first of several attempts began in 1529. To meet the crisis, the Monarchy established military buffer zones in present-day Croatia and Slovenia, intended to provide advanced warnings to Vienna of attacks originating from the south by Turkish forces, their vassal states, such as the Bosnians, and brigands. For protection along the border, Christian landholders built fortifications—castles, fortified manor houses and hilltop defensive positions—staffed by soldiers.

The fiefdom of Kostel was located in a military buffer zone bordering the Kupa River, on a narrow fertile plain that snaked through forest-covered hills. The fief's land area was not large, containing some fifty farming villages, as well as a castle. About six hundred inhabitants lived there at the end of the sixteenth century.

The "K" series of novels draw from actual historical events, and both the villages and surnames of the main characters are found in records of the era.

Book I
Devsirme
Fiefdom of Kostel

CHAPTER ONE

**Saint George's Day
Market Kostel
<u>Friday, April 24, 1694</u>**

Johannes Stefanich, elderly and white-haired, slowly climbed the steps to the Church of the Three Kings' bell tower to watch the activities below. The serfs were in a festive mood, as it was both market day and the annual celebration honoring Saint George, the martyred fourth-century Roman soldier who gave his life rather than renounce Christianity and embrace paganism.

Large crowds filled the narrow village lanes of Market Kostel, the township at the foot of the hilltop castle. Traders, who traveled the empire, exchanged goods and gossiped with local villagers. The backs of men and horses carried the sacks of wheat, bundled fodder, caged chickens, strings of dried herbs and embroidered aprons as trade goods while flasks of wine, bright linen cloth, woolen shawls, aprons, salt, trinkets and other goods lined peddler booths.

That day had begun just after first light. Each *hide*—seven to eight acres judged sufficient to support the household of a serf family—paid the tax of one sheep or two silver coins to Franz Josef Count Lamberg, Lord of Kostel and owner of the fiefdom's land. As tithe for the church, an additional lamb went to the bishop's flock. Count Lamberg's chief steward carefully recorded the name of each serf and his tax payment in the castle's tax records, as a local priest from the church looked on, making his own tally.

Carefully making his way down the wooden steps from the bell tower, Johannes joined village priests in their sanctuary at midday for their plain meal of lentil soup and bread spread with lard. Outside, he knew that traders and serfs shared meals of pork sausages, broiled over open cooking grills, freshly made bread, greens and sweet cakes. Other treats, purchased from the visiting vendors, added to the celebratory mood, as trading continued between villagers, local merchants and visitors. Sounds of merriment drifted from the crowd to those inside the church as beer and wine flowed in the marketplace, adding to the air of joviality.

He found the discussion about Saint George among the priests, too ecclesiastical and solemn, so he finished his meal, thanked the brethren and returned to the bell tower to watch and enjoy the activities of the crowd.

Below, laughing youngsters followed a man, attired in bright clothing. Chuckling to himself, Johannes watched the jester ogling people with a garishly painted, handheld mask, adorned with an impossibly large nose and huge bulging eyes, set beneath shaggy brows made from the coarse hair of a horse's tail. When the jester tapped an unsuspecting man or woman on the shoulder from behind, the kids and all standing about roared with laughter, at the startled, and even frightened expression, on the victim's face.

Priests wandered among the gathering, seeking donations by selling small wooden crosses strung on rawhide ties. The Catholic religion emphasized that temptations lurked everywhere. The holy men at the festival assured all that their talismans offered a way to ward off such evils with a mere donation of a silver coin. While doubts persisted about the heavenly power of the amulets, many locales were respectful of church doctrine, for most quaked at the thought of having unabsolved sins remaining following death and the accompanying punishment of residing in endless purgatory.

He noticed a young boy at one corner of the Church of the Three Kings, dancing about and holding a wooden figure above his head to draw the attention of passersby that it was for sale. It depicted Saint George astride a stallion—sitting proud and tall—while thrusting a spear into Satan, represented as a fire-breathing dragon. His woodcarving father sat on a three-legged stool beside him, bent over a block of pine, a sharp knife in his hand and shavings on the ground, as he diligently worked to create another figurine.

Nearby, soldiers from the castle strolled among the festive throng, alert for thieves whose sleight of hand relieved wealthy and poor of their purses. Celebrations of this type drew some men and women bent on wrongdoing, just as bees are attracted to fragrant flowers.

Three gaily-garbed men played a lively tune on a mandolin and a fipple flute in the town square fronting the church, while a third slapped a tambourine against his thigh, encouraging the crowd to clap in time with the music. The players accompanied four high-stepping couples, wearing brightly embroidered full and half-length tunics, leggings and vests complete with matching white blouses or shirts, also colorfully stitched. Each of the men wore a raised red hat with a long tassel of the same color. The women topped off their costumes with a crown of flowers. The gathered crowd laughed and enthusiastically kept time, as the couples performed a traditional folk dance.

Late in the afternoon on that sunny spring day, he watched people begin to move toward a grassy knoll at one end of the village. Most spread tarps on the ground and arranged themselves in comfortable positions, waiting for the featured event. Laughter greeted newcomers, and good-natured calls filled the air.

The clatter of horses and carriages announced the arrival of the titled nobles and their retinue, who took seats on cushioned chairs at the edge of the crowd. Twenty-one-year-old Count Lamberg, dressed in finery and hose, was the young Lord of the Castle. He sat beside a richly attired stranger. Johannes learned from a priest that the new man was Baron Johann Michael Androcha of Fiume, the major trading port on the Adriatic Sea. Outsiders always prompted curiosity and gossip, and many watched as the two men leaned closely together, apparently talking in hushed voices.

Despite his youthful age, all knew that Count Lamberg owned four domains, including Kostel. He had inherited the latter the previous year, upon the death of his stepfather, Count Langenmantl. Some claimed that the young man was considering selling one or more of his fiefdoms. Thus, the presence of Baron Androcha was more than a passing curiosity and raised interesting questions. Others dismissed the rumored sale of Kostel as foolishness. Surely, the young Count would not sell the province, where he had grown up following his adoption.

Johannes was not sure. He had heard talk and wondered if there would be an announcement later during this celebratory day. The fact that Baron Androcha sat next to the young Count could be telling.

The Parish Bishop arrived and sat in the gallery, dressed in a white tunic beneath a crimson full-length and armless robe. He rested on a high-backed, intricately carved wooden chair. His lay priests lounged near him, wearing plain, homespun woolen tunics, belted with a single cord tied around the waist.

As everyone watched and waited for the highlight event, the assembled throng grew restless and muted whispers drifted aloft on the light breeze. Still, Johannes Stefanich waited, heightening the anticipation of the crowd. He took pride in being renowned throughout the Kupa River Valley as one of the favorite traveling storytellers.

Johannes slowly made his way through the gathering. A hushed murmur greeted his arrival, as the crowd turned to watch him walk toward the high point of the knoll. Those already seated parted to make a path for him as he moved with a measured gait.

His tunic, of dyed white wool, draped over his lanky frame and hung down to his leather sandals. A simple slit in the middle of the garment allowed his head and lengthy beard to emerge. A sturdy leather strap knotted the garment at the waist, with one end dangling down to his knee. Loosely hanging sleeves, attached at the shoulders to the tunic with yarn ties, covered his arms. The springtime sun warmed the afternoon, and his open vest draped loosely over his thin shoulders. A flat woven straw hat completed his attire. From a distance, he knew it gave him the appearance of a golden halo hovering above him.

He looked neither left nor right during his unhurried walk and nodded to few along his path. He held a two-stringed gusle in one hand, an instrument with a round concave body and fettered neck. The other clutched a large shapeless sack.

The serfs sitting and lounging near the knoll stared curiously at him, as he slowly topped the rise and laid the instrument and pack aside. Stooping forward, he drew up the back and front hems of the tunic between his legs and stuffed the material beneath his leather belt, exposing his linen-wrapped legs. He placed the sack on the ground with great care, repositioning it once or twice, plumping and arranging its contents into a pillow. Then, he sat and made himself comfortable. In a practiced move, he stuffed his long beard inside his vest and rested the stringed instrument on one leg, cradling it in the crook of his arm.

Johannes stared at the ground for long moments, as though composing himself. He sensed the crowd's anticipation, as he, and others like him, were part of an oral tradition that spanned thousands of generations, handing down tales of valiant deeds and tragedies in the form of homilies, history addresses and lessons drawn from life's experiences.

He reached into a deep, hidden pocket in his tunic and drew out a soft leather flask. Slowly removing the stopper, he drank deeply. He wiped his mouth with the back of his hand and glanced at his audience, chuckling. Then, speaking in a booming voice filled with mirth, he said, "Our honored and noble gentry, holy fathers who grace us this day and serfs of this land, everyone knows the wisdom handed down through the ages. Wine is a gift given to all men from heaven above, but man's joy lies in drinking such a blessing." Pausing for only a moment, he continued,

"Which means, my friends, that wine makes you *strong* ... and water makes you *weak*."

The crowd applauded and laughed with him, delighting in the old, familiar phrase. Indeed, storytellers were also entertainers.

Johannes saw that the serfs seated before him wore their best woolen and linen clothes. Most colors were gray or white, the natural shades of the materials, with other colors mingled in such as brown, blue, and russet.

Women wore full-length tunics over a chemise or undertunic. Additionally, they wore square or rounded shaped bodices fastened in front with laces; these cut across the middle of their bosoms and were secure enough to contain even the fullest figure. Colorful headscarves adorned the heads of most women and older girls. With few exceptions, they also wore an apron tied around the waist; some were plain or pleated, while others were highly embroidered, with beautifully intricate stitching in bright colors. Widows dressed entirely in black, including their babushkas, as was the tradition.

Men also dressed in their finest thigh-length tunics, belted at the waist with a leather strap. Few wore the optional sleeves, as the day was warm. Many wore leather jerkins, a vest-like garment with elongated ends trailing down the split front opening. The typical clothing for leg coverings was to wrap them with strips of linen cloth; on that feast day, most wore the leggings. Headgear consisted of straw hats, or a fitted coif made from hemp, with ear coverings and strings ties that fastened the cap beneath the chin during colder periods; today, the strings hung loose.

Johannes bent his head toward the instrument, and his right hand flicked across the gusle's strings once and, immediately, a hushed and expectant silence fell upon the gathering. His fingers strummed the instrument again and then continued. The sound was not particularly melodic;

instead, it provided a distinct way to pace the rhythmic tempo of his homily.

Suddenly, Johannes looked up and stared at the crowd, swinging his piercing blue eyes from left to right, as the strumming of the gusle continued. He saw them all, yet his gaze never lingered on an individual. Many who knew him felt uncomfortable in his presence, for the man's piercing hypnotic stare had an inner quality and intensity. When aroused, some said that his glance could penetrate to the very essence of a man's soul. A few in the gathering involuntarily cringed, as his blue eyes raked their way. Others, in anticipation of his tale, found the pace of their breathing increase. There was no stir among the large crowd—not a cough or the impatient rustle of clothes—only total silence.

"My name is Johannes Stefanich," he said in a commanding voice. "I am better known throughout the land as Johannes, the Storyteller. I have traveled far and learned many things, during my long life. Some know my poems from former years, perhaps at the celebration last year, when I sang for several days. This time, my brethren, I recall the wise man from the East, who said~

> If you do not know the trees,
> You may be lost
> In the forest forever.
>
> But, God forbid,
> If you do not know the stories,
> You may forever be lost in life.

"You can learn how to find your own way from my poems. This afternoon, I recite the tale about the attack that occurred here, in this Fiefdom of Kostel. The uncivilized Turkish barbarians call their raids *devsirme*, their word for collecting or harvesting. I suppose that if you are a shepherd or farmer, the word *devsirme* is appropriate. When applied to forcibly kidnapping children, it becomes hideously vile—barbarism at its worst, leaving unbelievable heartbreak and devastating sorrow.

Long ago, an unknown barb stated it as a lament—

> Be damned, Sultan,
> Thrice be damned,
> For the evil, you have done,
> And the evil you still do.
>
> You catch and shackle the old,
> To steal the young as janissaries.
> Parents weep, their sisters and brothers, too,
> And, I cry until it pains me.
>
> As long as I live, I shall cry,
> And before long, it will be my son, too.

"All of us know that *desirme* means paying tribute in blood to the devil." Continuing, he intoned, "What was once in time..." Johannes paused for emphasis, before continuing in a singsong voice—

> I heard long ago
> And in this way
> Tell all to know

As the strumming kept time, he said, "We make our clothes, plow the land, raise our animals, feed our family and pray to the good Lord in heaven above. After a lifetime of hard work and paying our taxes, what is our legacy? What footprints do we leave behind to mark the fact that we once lived and walked the dusty roads of life?"

He paused once more to let the crowd ponder the question, still strumming the instrument's strings. Johannes broke the silence with a voice that roared like a lion, making some serfs who lounged too close, jump.

"Hear me, my brethren, for I will answer. It is our children. They alone rise to the worthiness of our persevering, for they are our *riches*. Anyone stealing that wealth from us is the worst kind of thief, denying us immortality through our offspring and those whom they beget. The Ottoman Empire's barbaric practice is the height of brutality and the reason that people fear and hate the Turkish raiders. Their attacks are fewer now, but when will they ever stop? To that, I have no answer."

He stared out at the crowd, sympathizing with the harshness and misery of their lives. As a youth, he was one of the very few given the opportunity to study theology at the University of Vienna under the tutelage of the Jesuits. He knew from his readings that slave labor had maintained vast agricultural estates for centuries while the Roman Empire flourished. With the Empire's demise, a feudalistic system replaced it that created new compacts between slaves working the land and the elite who were landowners. The agreement was straightforward—former slave patriarchs engaged in agricultural production, called serfs, received the right to work a hide and to pass that right to his eldest son, binding the holder to the land and, after that, to successor generations of eldest male progeny.

Thank God, we do not have any extensive and humanly demeaning slave trafficking among Balkan Christians like the Muslim heathens do in their lands, he thought. Even so, he was well aware that serfs were subject to the will of the landholder. The Lord's approval was required before the head of a hide could leave a fief permanently. Further, when the ownership of a fief changed, serfs continued to farm their same hides, which transferred land-bound families from one owner to another. His view was that this was simply slavery in another form.

Johannes had studied translated copies of the Qur'an and a compilation of the sayings of the Prophet Mohamed. He knew both prohibited slavery, yet Islamic religious scholars ruled that these passages applied only to those who followed and accepted Islam as their religion. This led to the creation and operation of active and extensive slave marketplaces in the Ottoman Empire for those who followed other religious beliefs—people referred to as "nonbelievers." He knew Christians were in this category.

His mind drifted for a few more moments as he continued his pause for dramatic panache.

Landholders were always responding to Vienna's demands for increased taxes. He knew well the burdens and misery this placed on the people and observed it in the horrific number of deaths among the young, such as the experiences here in Kostel.

Other practices had evolved, which buttressed the feudalistic structure, including social covenants, conditions and church doctrine. Such rules provided a framework for maintaining continuity and adherence. For example, the adoption of surnames in this part of the world began in the late 15th century. He realized that many serfs had delighted with the change, proudly responding, for instance, to "Ivan Spincic," instead of "Ivan, living near the bend of the river under the tall fir tree." For those collecting taxes, including church tithes, it was a boon, as it simplified the processes of levying and recording collections.

Still other doctrines supported the systemic order of society. Fiefdom owners and leaseholders, granted by the Hapsburg Monarchy, enacted and enforced local rules, established rights, opined on peasant marriages and when they felt compelled, attempted to impose their will on local priests and bishops.

Focusing his piercing blue eyes on his audience once more, Johannes continued. "Today, I sing of one such attack and Abdul Azim, the Turkish Janissary *Aga,* and commander of a Turkish horde, which descended upon Kostel over one hundred years ago, in the year of our Lord, fifteen hundred and eighty. Ungodly men, such as Aga Azim, practiced the devil's way, stealing our young Christian children, making them tributes in the service of the Sultan, while breaking the hearts of every parent, relative, and friend. With such evil deeds, men like Aga Abdul Azim deprived us of our reason to live and our wealth in this life. Further, woe to the brave father who opposed the kidnapping of his child; the Sultan of the Ottoman Empire, himself, decreed that such men possessed blood that was unworthy, and they were hung from the doorways of their homes.

"My tale is also one of courage on the part of two women who challenged the mighty Turkish force and, with their determination, struck a forceful blow. These were simple serfs, accustomed to the hard work of women living on hides, helping their family survive. Their remarkable determination, in the face of overwhelming obstacles, is part of this remarkable tale.

"It is, as my grandfather's grandfather said, who, as a young boy, witnessed the happenings in the village of Am Furtt, located a few miles upriver from where we rest this afternoon. It is a tale of paying the blood tax," he continued, gently plucking the two-stringed gusle.

> For all of thee
> I recite this homily.
> And reveal for ye
> Tales of one family.

On my father's knee
I heard long before.
More true it cannot be
Then Helena's war."

CHAPTER TWO

Brod na Kupi
June 1580

"Blessed be the Lord! May He save all of us on this day," Helena Klobucar pleaded to the sky above. "Petar, run, we must cross the river quickly to the village and help save the children."

Her husband made no move; the expression of shock evident on his face. His hands trembled uncontrollably, as he removed his hat and ran one through his thinning white hair.

Helena knew exactly what the bonfire signal on the hill meant. It forewarned that Turkish raiders were sweeping north again, traveling up the valley from the crossroad village of Delnice, twelve miles to the south. She pictured what was occurring along the way—raiders on horseback overrunning small farms and rural hamlets—just as they had done previously over the decades.

Hearing no response, Helena shrieked, "Mary, Mother of God! Hurry, Petar, we must hide the children, for the Devil, himself, comes this time." She moved as quickly as possible on aged legs. Her face was white and etched with fear. It was late afternoon. She paused and anxiously looked over her shoulder at the flames on the distant hill, screening her eyes with her hand. She also saw her husband squinting at the blaze.

"I see no yellow smoke," he finally announced. "It means that it is not a large force coming toward us." He was referring to an attack years earlier, when the Turks came through the area after attacking Vienna, with an army regiment numbering over six thousand."

"No yellow smoke?" Helena repeated, knowing that the boys on the hilltop mimicked the same warning they saw farther to the south. If local boys saw yellow smoke, they added a powder to the hot flames that created a cloud of the same color. "Thank the Holy Father," she said, making the sign of the cross. "Even so, we must quickly cross the river to Am Furtt. A small Turkish horde is just as dangerous as a large army to us."

Villagers prepared dry firewood each spring and stacked a fresh supply on the lookout hill. Older boys stood watch during the day, always watching for any signs from the south. When it occurred, news of advancing riders spread rapidly across the rural countryside, as torches lighted one hilltop fire after another.

Still, the old man did not move. He apparently was stunned and still trying to process the reality confronting everyone in the Kupa River Valley.

"My husband, why are you standing there? Are you rooted to the ground like a tree?" Helena asked, concern evident in her voice. "We must warn everyone in Am Furtt and move them quickly to the cave, deep in the forest—particularly the young ones. They must be hidden from the devil soldiers!"

Helena had often heard the stories about Turkish Janissary soldiers from the time she was very young. This elite corps from the Ottoman Empire exacted terror and chaos every four to five years during raids along the frontier—burning, looting, raping, killing and kidnapping—as the well-mounted troops used their gleaming, thirty-inch *yatagan* swords to slash through any opposition. The distinctive blades had always fascinated and frightened her. The single edge of tempered steel had a signature forward curve, complete with handles created from a variety of materials—bone, ivory, horn or silver—and attached to the tang, the slender handle-end of the metal.

The Turks were devil-like men to the serfs, pursuing *devsirme*. They sought young children as tributes for the Ottoman Empire—much as a herdsman gathers scattered sheep for his flock—ripping pre-puberty boys and girls from the arms of desperate mothers and fathers. Kostelians had a different term for *devsirme*—they called it paying *the blood tax*.

Helena knew the stories about the dozens of past assaults on the fiefdom. At celebrations and gatherings, elders frequently spoke in dark terms recalling prior attacks, until the terror became ingrained and cold fear gripped everyone's heart at the mere mention of the dreaded event. Seeing the warning fire on the hill rekindled those fears and the accompanying remembrances—sadness, anger, bewilderment and despair. Neither she nor anyone else had an explanation for the reasons behind the brutal kidnappings nor what happened to the children—the young ones simply disappeared forever from the arms of their parents. Now, it was about to happen once more.

She shouted even louder, "Do you hear me, old man? Run! The life of our young great grandson depends on hiding him from the horsemen." Teetering, Helena aimed her boot for a well-placed kick at Petar's behind. "For the love of God, move your old legs, my husband!" she shouted, exasperated.

He roused himself and finally began running, loudly shouting to his wife, "The *kučkin sin*, bastards, come our way again! When will we be free of their wicked curse? And when will the Lord strike down these heathens—and send them to the hot infernos of hell?"

"Blasphemy will cause Satan to burn your soul, my husband, but it will not bring God's wrath this instant nor will it stop the Turks," Helena panted, as she struggled with the rapid pace. Thinking as she hurried along, she continued, "Surely, the warning fires are visible to the soldiers at the castle. They should already be moving this way to confront the dreaded enemy."

"More likely, they are wondering how to protect the arse of Count Petar Erdody and their own by sitting behind the thick, stone walls of Kostel Castle."

Turning a corner, they moved quickly through the dusty lanes of Brod na Kupi, a town of size located on a river variously called *Kupa* or *Kupi*. The name Brod na Kupi translated to "town on the Kupi River," and it was located in a fiefdom that neighbored Kostel. Brod was the largest trading community by far in the area with several hundred inhabitants.

As they hurried, the two elderly serfs glanced at the town's imposingly tall Zrinski Castle, with its high defensive walls of stone. The castle tower was complete with narrow vertical openings in the sidewalls, called arrow loops, which allowed bowmen and musketeers to fire and repel the attacking force while remaining sheltered from return fire. Therefore, the raiders avoided getting within range of the soldiers housed in the stone fortress. Helena and Petar knew from previous experiences that the few Zrinski defenders would not engage the Turks unless the stronghold came under direct attack.

Petar and Helena turned off the main road and took the lane to the ferry. The barge was at the landing, at a point where the *Kubica*, a small stream, intersected the main river.

Helena was dismayed to see the crowd that was already jockeying for position at the loading dock. It seemed that half of Brod had the same idea—crossing the river and placing it between themselves and the advancing raiders. "Petar, where are all these people going?" she asked, in amazement.

Without responding, the old man stepped aboard the barge and turned toward the crowd. Raising his hands high, he shouted, "Stop! You will sink the boat or tip it over for there are too many of you. *STOP—STOP I SAY, AND LISTEN TO ME!*"

The crowd quieted at the sound of his voice.

"We must flee the Turkish horror that is coming our way," one man hollered.

Another yelled, "Yes, ferryman, take us across the Kupa, for the love of God! Have mercy on my young ones and us!"

"And do what," Petar replied sternly. "The signal on the hill indicates it is a small force moving towards us. That means two things: They will not attack Brod because the town is too large and has too many people. Secondly, the Turks will cross the river right here at the Am Furtt ferry crossing. And, there is nothing to stop them, short of burning the barge."

From somewhere, a shrill voice challenged, "We all know that the other side of the river is safer than staying in town."

"What makes you think that you will be safer when you are going in the same direction as the Turks?" Petar responded, curtly. "All of you know that there is only one barge to cross the water for many miles up or down the river. Right here, this is the place where the Turks will load their wagons on the ferry to reach the other side."

There was silence—one of anguish and despair—as the old man's words echoed in the minds of those at the riverbank.

The ferryman continued, "And if you and your family make it across, what will you do then? Will you hide in one of the sheds across the river that my neighbors and I use for storing grain and fodder? What if the soldiers trap you there like mice eating cheese in the cellar? I can tell you this—you are not welcome to hide in the attic of my house, for I will already be there," he chided.

Another voice demanded, "Stop wasting time, old man! Do you have another suggestion?"

"For the love of God, people—think of what you are doing! Go in the other direction, south to the hills—where it will be difficult for the Turks to find you in the thick forests. My wife and I have to cross the river to reach our village. But, all of you, run that way!" he said, pointing toward the forested hills.

The crowd stood stock still for an instant; then, in mass, they turned and headed toward the trees.

Stepping aboard the boat, Helena said, "I have untied us from the shore. Pull, my husband. Pull hard on the line. The children are in grave danger!"

Spitting into the palms of his hands for a firmer grip, Petar seized the draw rope tightly. He gave a mighty tug, which moved the ferry into the current.

Am Furtt

Petar and Helena tied off the barge and hurried across plowed fields. In their haste, their route took them through a meadow where they parted a small herd of grazing sheep. The two elderly people forded a shallow stream and passed boxes containing frames of honeybees and then they crossed a field planted in wheat, making sure to remain on a worn footpath to minimize trampling the growing crop. Winded, they arrived in the center of Am Furtt, their small farming hamlet.

The beating of an iron spike against the bottom of a metal pot sounded the alarm, as the signal flames on the hill were clearly visible. Children screamed, and adults shouted in panic. Some men and women bore huge bundles on their heads or strapped across their shoulders, containing their possessions. With the use of sticks, most men and older children herded animals—cows, sheep, goats, oxen and horses—toward the forest. Some also clutched wildly flapping chickens by the legs in their free hand, in an attempt to save as much as possible. Pigs remained in their pens, as the Islamic religion prohibited their consumption.

Helena stood beside a small sanctuary dedicated to the Virgin Mary, watching the panic and chaos that gripped villagers. She saw her grandson, Steffan, and his wife, Maria, carrying baby Anton, and running toward the river, likely seeking to conceal themselves inside one of the village's several drying sheds.

"Come back, Steffan!" Helena called to them. "The Turkish raiders know those hiding places. Surely, you remember the stories of the evil ones thrusting their halberd lances into the fodder in search of our people. Go the other way—to the forest. Go toward the hills to the north, cross *Černá Potok*, Black Creek, and hurry to the large cave behind the waterfall! We will shelter there and wait for the castle soldiers—but be quick!"

The young people stopped and looked at each other, then followed Helena's directions, recognizing her prominence as a respected elder, as well as the matriarchal force in their family and the village. Additionally, she was Steffan's grandfather wife, and he was the *suppan* or mayor of the village.

Helena turned around and rushed into her white-washed stone house, entering a large room with a round hearth in the center. The aroma of baked bread greeted her, mingled with the odd but distinctive fragrances of boiled turnips, cabbage and burning juniper. The latter was a local remedy, said to ward off a dreaded disease contracted from river water.

There was another room through a doorway on the right, which the whole family shared as a bedroom. Lighting a candle and picking up a knife, Helena entered the second room. Inside were wooden beds with straw-stuffed mattresses, wooden wardrobes and, against one wall, a small cabinet. Moving it aside, she knelt on the hard packed floor, although this pained her knees. She pried loose a stone block from the wall using the knife and withdrew a leather pouch. Impatiently, she shook it and heard the clink of coins.

Helena flipped up the edge of her apron, then the hem of her tunic and tied the strings of the leather purse to a linen band that she wore around her waist. She positioned the pouch so that it hung down the back of her leg. This permitted her to walk, or hurry, without interference, yet it kept the family silver out of sight.

Grasping a quilt from a straw tick, she rushed back to the kitchen and spread it on the table. She tossed a slab of bacon, two loaves of bread—made fresh that morning—and other assorted items from the larder onto the blanket. Pulling together two corners of the blanket, she tied them together securely. Next, she tied the other corners, forming a tight bundle and hurried out of the door, placing the pack on her head.

She stopped and turned around some distance from her home, trembling and staring at it, looking at the house number—7—plainly visible above the door. *I wonder if it will still be standing when I return. More importantly, what is to become of my family, if the Turks find us—and Maria and her young boy?* Sighing, she shook off her dread and passed other houses clustered along several dirt lanes in the small village.

A long stone's throw would strike most of the two dozen dwellings that comprised the centralized and compact settlement of Am Furtt. A garden and an orchard were behind every farmhouse. Outbuildings and a pen for the family's pigs were usually near the back of the property, often behind a wood stake fence.

Everyone considered a farm incomplete without a vineyard; hence, every hide had one, with vines elevated on tree limbs. Hemp cords stretched between the uprights. In the spring, farmers tied spreading vines to the cords, which kept the fruit off the ground and prevented it from rotting. Each household crushed and fermented the harvested grapes in the fall and made the family's annual supply of wine.

Communal fields of grain and pastures surrounded the village on three sides beyond the backyards. These extended down to the river while forested hills bordered the upslope edge of the village.

As Helena turned toward the woods, other villagers held flaming torches high, lighting the way in the darkening forest. Terrified for her family and great-grandson, she looked eastward, desperately hoping to see soldiers riding hard from the castle to protect them. With none in sight, she sighed dejectedly and hustled after her fleeing neighbors into the thick stands of trees.

Running with Anton in her arms, Maria asked Steffan, "Are we going to the same cave where everyone hid the last time? I remember it as being large."

"Yes, it is big enough to accommodate all the villagers in this part of the Kupa Valley."

"We will all be trapped inside if the Turks follow and discover us. There is only one opening!"

Exasperated, Steffan snapped, "What do you prefer—being lanced in a drying shed or taking a chance on the cave?"

As they hurriedly continued through the trees, Maria said, "Steffan, do not be angry with me. My nerves are on edge, and I fear that something will happen to Anton. I am also afraid of what may happen to you, as well as to the others in the village."

"Well, your concerns might as well include yourself, dear wife. These fiends are rarely kind and gentle with any women they come across, particularly those who are young and attractive—such as you."

Startled, Maria tossed him a confused look. "You sound so cold as though you do not care. How can you think such hideous thoughts and be so callous."

"I care very much! You and I have heard the same stories many times, and we know what occurs during such raids. The marauders are filthy pigs, who steal little ones and terrorize everyone. That includes raping multiple women and pillaging villages, as well as killing anyone standing in their way. The men of the village are powerless to resist the attackers, and none of us can even defend our houses and hides. There are too few of us, and we have little in the way of weapons. As you know, most villagers have no soldiering experience. That is why we all run—just like a flock of sheep before a pack of wolves!" he commented bitterly.

Exhausted from the fast pace while carrying the baby, Maria paused a moment to catch her breath, as a chill of fear ran down her back.

"Keep going," Steffan said, returning to assist her by taking Anton from her. "It is vital that we reach the cave before the Turks cross the river."

CHAPTER THREE

In the last light of day, Abdul Azim, the Commanding *Aga*, accompanied by his raiding party of fifty men, concluded his fifth prayer of the day and recited the Muslim words of witness:

> "There is no true God but Allah, and
> Muhammad is the Messenger of God."

He removed his tall, white Janissary hat and knelt at the edge of the river, cupping a handful of water from the fast-flowing waterway to quench his thirst. Leaning back, Azim lounged against a pillow near the campfire, holding a lambskin map loosely in his lap. However, his thoughts that evening were elsewhere, as his brown eyes gazed across the Kupa River.

I completed my Five Pillars of Faith of Islam earlier this year when I returned from the pilgrimage to Mecca, he reflected. *Everyone should travel to the holy site at least* once in his lifetime. It is truly awe-inspiring. And, with all my being, I will continue to recite the testimony of faith, support the needy, pray five times a day facing Mecca, and fast from dawn to sundown during Ramadan—the ninth month of the lunar calendar of the Muslim year.

He ran a hand through his thick dark hair, removed his leather belt and rearranged his green caftan about him for greater comfort. He was tall with a well-developed body from years of military training and service. His face and sideburns were clean-shaven.

We have made good progress, reaching the Kupa by tonight, he thought. *Darkness is a good time for continuing our raids, as it fills serfs with even greater terror and panic, like those awaiting our arrival across the river. Still, it is better to cross this broad and swift-moving water in daylight. I will have some of my men swim across in the morning, following the current and floating on goatskins filled with air. They can bring the toll barge to this side of the river, which will allow us to send the heavy wagons over safely, while my troops forage the villages ahead, searching for serfs and food.*

My information is that the Zrinski Castle soldiers have never been a problem on our previous journeys, and we have already harvested little ones from that fief. The guards sitting behind those stone walls are probably quaking in their boots.

Afterward, it will not take us many days to move through the entire fiefdom of Kostel, as it has no large towns such as Brod. The map indicates that a man can travel across the domain in less than a day on foot. I will have my men create a divergence so that the Kostel soldiers remain in the castle and do not confront us.

The little ones selected on this devsirme trip will be fortunate, indeed, and will become skilled at their assigned tasks. They will become loyal to Islam and Sultan Murad III, much as my Janissary troopers and I are.

He paused to consider the irony. *Here I am,* he thought, *leading my men to harvest young children, just as others took me from my village and parents fifteen years ago.*

I know all serfs fear us, yet the collected immature boys will each have an opportunity to become a Janissary warrior, or become educated as clergy in the church of the Greeks. Still others can train to undertake government positions. During the journey here, one mother tried to bribe me with silver coins and pleaded with me to take her son, believing that he would have a chance for a better life. And praise Allah, she was right. Still, I rejected him. Who needs a little one with the strings of a woman's apron binding him?

It would be marvelous if one of the boys from this trip became a high official, Abdul Azim thought, *or even, could I be so blessed, a Grand Vizier, second only to the Sultan Himself, and conducting the affairs of state. My heart would burst with pride if such a wonder took place. Only Allah knows the future, yet I hear that such occurrences have happened in the past.*

His mind wandered, thinking about other possibilities. *The boys will learn about Islam and languages as they become men. They will also learn about geography and mathematics. Then, the fittest will undergo years of training for warfare. Janissary means "new soldier," and that is what they will become. Among all our armies, we are the greatest warriors of all. It results from our excellent training, and the strict discipline maintained throughout our close, elite corps. All our enemies quake at the thought of facing us on the battlefield. We are the battle-tested point of the spear for our Sultan.*

The young girls take other paths. They will learn the duties of becoming servants in the Sultan's many households, perhaps as chambermaids in the harem. Others will become skilled as concubines, learning the intricate art of pleasing and gracing the beds of noblemen. Maybe a beautiful girl from this very devsirme will one day become a favorite of a future Sultan ... or even achieve the supreme harem rank of wife to the Sultan. The concubine system always produces many heirs, which assures that a Sultan's line continues uninterrupted. Ha, in the world of the Christians, one barren marriage or death of a male heir interrupts the succession of a dynasty and leads to chaos.

His mind fancied an even grander scheme, as he continued daydreaming. *Perhaps, one girl collected on this trip will attain the rank of Queen Mother—wife of one and birth mother of his successor. I dream big thoughts, but this, too, has happened to white female slaves.*

I will again offer a prayer in the morning that such a blessing can befall me from one of the young ones harvested on this journey. If Allah grants it, so it shall be.

His second in command, Tasar, approached and sat beside him, near the fire. "Peace be unto thee, Aga Azim." He was short, with a bull neck and broad chest. His legs resembled tree stumps, and the man's hip girth matched his other proportions.

"And unto thee, my friend." *He is a superb and loyal fighter. It is an honor to have him at my side in any battle.* Unlike his own brown eyes, Tasar's were blue, and the glow of the campfire reflected off his shaved head. His leathery facial was shaved, but it appeared parched from too many days of exposure to the sun and wind.

Pointing, Tasar said, "Behold the meadows and fields of grain across the river. In this last light of day, it looks like lush green gardens, framed by the hardwood and pine forests on the hills beyond. It is beautiful, is it not, Aga?"

"Indeed."

"We saw the peasants' bonfire on the hill today, so they know that we are coming. The soldiers at the castles have surely seen the warning. What do you expect them to do?"

"We shall see, but I venture that our ride up the valley has been so swift that it has immobilized the Zrinski Castle Lord and his soldiers. I believe the same will be true at Kostel Castle. You recall that we had an army of many thousands of troops some years back, when we attacked Vienna, then later Gottschee just thirty miles north of here, before returning to cross the river at this location. The bonfires likely indicate that we are smaller in number this time, but the questions at the castles remain—what is the size of our force and what is our destination?"

"And, we saw no villagers, when we came through Am Furtt some years ago," Tasar remembered. "So no fuss was made when we helped ourselves to their chickens and grain."

"Yes," Azim commented. "I believe that we will not be troubled by the soldiers from either castle, and we can reap and collect our harvests without undue concern."

Tasar nodded. "Aga, we already have one hundred twenty-seven children under guard, with still another forty or fifty to levy on this trip. When will you call for the initial examination of the little ones?"

"Perhaps after we turn south from this fiefdom," Azim replied.

Azim knew the process well. The evaluation would begin with the troop's slaves stripping off the young ones' clothes and bathing them in the river. Two of his men, experienced in such matters, then assessed each one, looking for any illness, infestation, unsightly birthmarks, deformities or anything that might disqualify a captive child. It also assured that all the girls were virgins. Upon the troop's return to Istanbul, a final examination would take place. Any rejection there would reflect poorly on his leadership and judgment.

After the inspection, the slaves in his troop will dress the captives in new red robes, clothes that are more fitting for young ones destined to serve Allah and Sultan Murad, he thought. *Additionally, the bright color makes runaways easier to recapture.*

Beheading was the unenviable reward for any young captive failing the detailed examination. No excuses sufficed. The Turks merely flung the body into the river and placed the head in a linen sack, along with those of others who were unworthy and had resisted the Janissary's advance. Each would find a home at the end of a sharp stake driven into the ground, marking the route of his troop's departure from Christian lands. Instilling fear in peasants and serfs along the frontier buffer zone between the Hapsburg and Ottoman lands was always part of *devsirme* marches.

Tasar interrupted his thoughts. "At this moment, the infidels must be hiding under their beds, quaking at what awaits them in the morning."

Nodding, Azim said, smiling, "Remember our orders, Tasar. We are to take neither first born males nor the sons of merchants or Jews."

"Why are such restrictions placed on our collections, Aga?"

"For one thing, the rules assure that our flock of serfs keeps breeding to supply sons and daughters for future harvests."

"I can see the wisdom in that."

"Each head of the house or serf patriarch is assigned the right to work a plot of land, which continues to pass from father to eldest son, generation after generation. That is why we exclude the eldest male children from our *devsirme*. Secondly, there is no slave marketplace in the infidel's feudal system, as is our custom. All the serfs remain on their parcel and transfer with the land when one Lord sells a fiefdom to another. I do not know the answer regarding your question about excluding the children from craftsmen and merchant families. A commander once told me he assumed the rule was established to minimize disruption in Christian villages."

Azim's second nodded, taking in the information while still showing a quizzical look on his face.

"As you know, Tasar, all nations, tribes and ethnic groups that are conquered by our Ottoman Empire must convert to Islam as laid down by the true prophet, Mohamed. Afterward, self-rule is permitted, provided they remain loyal to the Sultan.

"Mohamed stated that Jews and Muslims had common roots and referred to the two as 'Abrahamic religions.' Both reference Abraham, Noah, Jesus and Moses in their holy books and share certain rituals. Over the centuries, the religions choose different paths. Even so, many Jews retain the right to practice Judaism in the way they wish. Given the sizeable number within our empire, it is best not to upset sensibilities."

"I understand what you say, but . . ."

"Look, Tasar, we are loyal to the Sultan we serve. Those commands come from him through his Grand Vizier. Hence, as loyal white slaves, we obey."

"All right, I will not argue the matter further."

Both men turned silent, lost in their thoughts.

Then, his second officer continued, "Before we left Istanbul, I heard there were more than thirty thousand Janissaries who comprise our elite corps of warriors."

"Yes, it is quite a formidable group, is it not? I also heard from one of our esteemed scholars that, in total, there are currently over one hundred thousand white slaves in the empire. Can you even imagine such a number?"

"Impressive, is it not? Those born to Christian parents now have the joy of Islamic teachings. And, of course, there are all the other slaves in the empire, particularly from Africa."

Both men lapsed into silence again.

Tasar finally asked, "At the slave marketplace, which slaves fetch the highest price?"

"I am told that whites sell for more than blacks, with attractive white virgin girls going for three-and-four-times the cost of a male."

"Hmm, interesting," his second in command replied. "I also hear there is quite a market for white eunuchs these days. Is that right?"

"I believe so. A slave trader told me that castrated white slaves are in demand and command ten times the price of those uncut. I wonder how many of our little ones from this trip will become eunuchs, after feeling the full sting of a blade?"

". . . and survive," Tasar added, with a wry chuckle.

Grinning and slapping his leg in mirth, Azim added, "As the Coptic priests say, make the slice even with the belly. Of course, each of the boys will have his foreskin removed, as it is our custom."

Tasar continued his thoughtful gaze across the river.

Noticing his friend's concentration, Azim inquired, "What is on your mind, my friend?"

"If I had been cut, perhaps I would not have such stirrings, as I look to the other side of the river. Aga, I wish to scatter my seed among the fair, young women over there. I observe that many serf women have deep bosoms and generous backsides." Chuckling, he added, "These qualities are quite appealing to hard men like us, who have been in the saddle for so long. It is pleasing to contemplate, is it not, Aga?"

Silence overcame them once more.

The observation touched a sensitive nerve with Azim. Through the centuries, one measure of enforcing discipline in the ranks of Janissary slaves was the strict prohibition against intimacy with females. He knew that the rule pushed many of his brethren toward sexual follies with boys and other men, and though he had participated, it left him wanting. Before leaving Istanbul, reliable sources said that a change in the policy was coming soon—one that would permit Janissaries to have sex with women, perhaps even to marry.

His officer interrupted the silence again. "We both know that changes are coming for Janissaries, which will be in effect by the time we return to Istanbul. You will not hold us to our pledge of abstinence with women for the rest of this trip, will you? I know that our half-dozen Janissary long to till some female furrows. I can hardly keep them in check."

My God, I live for such a change, myself, Azim thought. *The new rules will be effective by our return. Why should I continue to deny my troops the pleasures of bedding peasant women, while the Bosnian ruffians riding with us spill their seed? It obviously is on Tasar's mind. It will be thrilling for my Janissaries, and for me,* he thought, *to debauch as many women on this journey that attract us, as time and opportunity permit.*

"You are right, Tasar," Azim finally replied. "See that the order passes to the men. But, hear me well; first, we secure our location and then see to the children and food to supply our journey. Afterward, the men can have their way with the women." Smirking, he added, "Besides, it means more young white slaves for our Sultan in the future, does it not?"

"Excellent deduction, my Aga," Tasar answered.

Thinking on the matter and staring into the campfire flames, Azim made a personal decision. *Spilling my seed in Christian heathen lands is a way to serve my Sultan, so future blood tax harvests carry the spirit of a great Janissary—me! What could be more fitting?*

With a chuckle he said. "Tasar, we continue at first light in the morning with the task of gathering our human levy."

As was their routine, they turned to the meal that slaves set before them. Both men relished and delighted in their supper of yogurt, dried fruit and skewered kebabs of roasted lamb, washed down with goat's milk.

Unspoken, they also savored visions of dark-haired women, shapely female bosoms and buttocks and having the opportunity, for the first time in their lives, to release their restrained, pent-up passions with a woman. It was waiting for them. All they had to do was cross to the other side of the Kupa River.

CHAPTER FOUR

Several torches provided dim light in the large cave, as Maria Klobucar cradled her four-month-old son, Anton, rocking him to calm and sway him asleep. Her state of mind, however, was highly agitated, as she thought of the approaching Turkish soldiers and the possibility of losing her son to such evil monsters. She heard people whispering, wondering where the castle guards were. Surely, they were on their way. Am Furtt was the only Kupa River crossing for many miles in either direction, and all could guess that the Turks would cross there.

Trying to steel her nerves, her eyes darted about in the dim torchlight and her breath quickened. She sensed that others had similar worries in the semi-darkness, and the collective apprehension seemed palpable.

Her eyes searched for Steffan's grandmother, the woman they both called Nana, hoping that the family matriarch would join her. If anyone could soothe Maria, she was the one. While Petar headed the household as the family patriarch, things took on urgency in the Klobucar farmhouse, when Helena made up her mind.

Nana Helena was not in the cave at that moment, which seemed strange. Rather, Maria saw Steffan and Petar near the entrance, talking with other men from the village. *What is there to discuss,* she silently questioned. *Either the Turks will find us—or not. Other than some staves, bows and hayforks, our weapons are no match for the Turk's pikes, swords and muskets. All we can do now is wait!*

With no one to console her, Maria's mind wandered in the dim light. She quaked at the tales of previous raids, just as Steffan had said, and the destruction and killing, followed by the abduction of young boys and girls. *Why, in the name of the Holy Father, do the Turks have the need for such barbarism and steal so many children over the years? Good Lord in heaven above, what do they do with all of them?* The more she pondered the possible reasons, the more alarmed and distraught she became.

Maria was not a strong believer in fate or myths, preferring to rely on her religious beliefs for comfort and guidance. She had feared being kidnapped by Turks or Muslim brigands as a young girl. Grimacing, she remembered one of the threats that many mothers used, including her own, to frighten a child who skirted daily chores. "The next time the Turks are here," they would typically say, "I will hand you to them as they ride by like evil trolls from hell. And, most likely, they will roast you for their evening supper!" It was a chilling threat for the young ones. Now, her concern was for her infant. *Surely, the Turks do not eat them,* Maria reasoned. *That would be too fiendish, even for the Turkish bearers of evil.* Still, her question remained unanswered.

She recalled many occasions, such as the feast of St. George's holy day the previous month. Villagers gathered at the parish church for the tithing. Late in the day, after everyone had feasted, talk always turned to the terrible marauders and the abduction of young children. The men drank wine or *rakia*—the potent colorless liquor, fermented and distilled from the dregs of wine production—and they whispered dark tales about farms being pillaged, people killed by the Janissary's razor-sharp swords or the rape of village women. Even if a traveling storyteller was not present at these celebrations, elders repeated the tales, passing on lessons in the oral tradition and communicating in a manner that was older than antiquity.

Remembering the stories, she knew that the Turks had no interest in her Anton at his present age, as he was too young. Even so, during raids with fast-charging horses and swinging swords, anything could happen. She trembled at the thought, and she hugged the boy closer to her.

An equally frightening question arose as her mind turned to what could be in store for village women later that day. *Rape and abuse of women always seem to occur when raiders come through a Christian area. Perhaps, a Turk just selects a woman, throws her on the ground and that is all there is to it,* she guessed. *What will become of me? Steffen said he thinks I am still fair in my looks. I get nods and winks from men at festivals—sometimes even a surreptitious pinch or grope in a crowded marketplace lane. Maybe the first man who finds me will take advantage and lift my tunics. Or, will it be a dozen of them, all lined up, waiting to take their turn?* She shuddered at either prospect, revolted by the thought. *Maybe, the leader assigns women according to the rank of his men or for former brave deeds. How will Steffan react if that is my fate? What can he do, with a musket or sword pointed at his chest?*

She had slept with only one man—Steffan. Their wedding night proved somewhat disappointing, as consuming too much *rakia* assured that her new husband was ill during their first night together after his friends drunkenly deposited him on the bed. Gradually, the newlyweds became more familiar with each other, and then she became pregnant. That ended their perfunctory sexual dalliances in the single bedroom, where eight had slept, before Steffan's brothers and sisters had left for homes elsewhere.

Of course, she knew about intercourse and conception. After all, she had lived on a farm all her life. Further, a few old men sometimes told erotic stories about men and women fornicating, particularly after rounds of wine or rakia loosened their tongues and inhibitions. Then, there were also the old shrews on the dusty lanes of Brod, who loudly recited coarse tales, which always made her blush as she crossed herself in supplication.

Maria could not shake a feeling of dread at what the sunrise might bring, with such thoughts swirling in her head. *Some man, smelling of sweat and horses, may drag me down in a field. I will resist, of course. Afterward, if I am still alive, what will the Lord think of me, when I am sullied by such heathens and have sinned? What will the priests at the parish church in Fara say following my confessional? Can my soul ever be cleansed? Can I ever look forward to rejoicing in heaven in the afterlife, while still carrying the stain of losing my mortal to the barbarians? Oh, sweet Jesus, in Heaven above, please watch over my family! I beseech thee. Spare us from the horror that may soon be upon all of us,* she prayed, bowing her head and tightly closing her eyes.

Time passed slowly. Maria's many questions and doubts left her with a high flush, and the pace of her breathing was faster than normal. Looking around the cave, she was relieved to see that no one took notice of her dilemma. There was still no sign of Helena, and both Steffan and Petar had disappeared from the cave opening.

Her thoughts turned again to Steffan and their marriage. She was from Vas, the next hamlet along the road eastward. It was a farming village like Am Furtt, but smaller. Steffan was nearly twenty-four, and she had just turned twenty-one. She had noticed him many times at Sunday church services and festivals, but he seemed less aware of her. Then, the previous year, they had worked side-by-side in the wheat fields, as neighbors helped each other during the consecutive weeks of a single yearly harvest in the entire river valley.

Afterward, Steffan stopped at her house twice when he was on his way to cut firewood in the forest. Her mother always arranged for an adult from the family or village to be nearby. While she enjoyed their brief talks, in truth, it made little difference which man she preferred or hoped to marry. Parents traditionally negotiated marriage arrangements for their children. It was a fundamental responsibility in the extended *familija* of a patriarchal, top-down societal order.

Maria remembered the first day that Helena and Petar Klobucar visited her parents and began discussing a dowry. Steffan's parents had died some years earlier during an outbreak of a strange cough and illness. Therefore, it was natural that his grandparents fulfilled the task of negotiating the marriage contract for his bride, and particularly the dowry.

Everyone dressed in their finest clothing, and she knew that her parents were nervous about the upcoming discussions. She was not sure that the talks centered on her, for she had two sisters, one of whom was older and first in line for an arranged marriage. Waiting outside her home, she strained to hear and was pleasantly surprised when she overheard her name mentioned.

Through the open door, she saw her mother serve a traditional meal to the honored visitors. Maria recalled that Petar sat down at the table with a bowl of mushroom soup before him, together with slices of freshly made bread, a staple of every meal, and lard as a spread. He tucked into the meal with gusto. He, like her father, had an appetite derived from years of long days and hard work on his farm. "*Dobro,*" he commented, "Good!"

Wild boar stew followed, and glasses of white wine accompanied the entire meal. It was the drink of choice for guests, as home brewed beer and milk were too common, and water was only for children. Next, her mother served Helena. Only then did she set out food for her husband. It was a tradition that guests ate first, beginning with the eldest man. Further, women served males in the family next, in the order of their age, followed by women and girls.

When the visitors finished eating the main meal, her mother served *palačinki* for dessert—thinly rolled pancakes filled with strawberry preserves and sweet soft cheese—and she set a bottle of *rakia* on the table. She made sure the glasses were clean, by giving them a final wipe with the apron tied around her waist.

Talks continued over a two-week period, and both sets of families exchanged visits to discuss the dowry. Neither Maria nor Steffan took part in the discussions, and they were not in in the house. Rather, both had their chores and work to do in the fields, while local neighbors watched, laughed and gossiped—then merrily relayed every detail that had transpired to each of them.

Her family made a case for a modest dowry, noting that Maria was strong, well skilled in farming chores, such as milking cows and goats, made tasty cheese and had helped raise her younger brothers and sisters. Both her mother and father raved about her cooking skills. All were important qualities in a wife. At one point, as Maria strained to hear, her father noted, "Coarse and calloused hands—those are a young woman's best dowry." She knew that was a phrase always spoken by the bride's parents, seeking to reduce the size of their daughter's dowry.

Glancing beyond the open door, she heard her father continue. "Maria is an excellent worker. You know, Helena, a woman carries three corners of every farm on her back, then she helps her husband with the fourth." Maria smiled, having heard that same comment many times before.

In turn, Steffan's grandparents spoke highly about his ability to wield the long scythe, mowing an impressive full dome of hay each day during harvest time. They also noted that he could lift two large sacks of grain over his head, a feat of strength that was admirable. Left unsaid was the young man's feudal right to work the Klobucar's productive hide when Petar died. Steffan father, Josip, was the first son of Petar and Helena, and with his death years earlier, the generational right would someday flow to Steffan after Petar's passing.

In one area, Maria knew there was little argument—the high regard afforded the Klobucar family. Petar was the mayor of his village. All Kostelians knew and respected the family as operators of the ferry. Even townsmen of Brod held them in the same regard. After all, Count Petar Erdody, the Lord of Kostel Castle, had first granted the Klobucar family a license to operate the Kupa River ferry and collect his tolls many years earlier. Helena or Petar made a point of reciting the number of times people requested them to act as godparents for infants born in their village and even by parents living in Brod, as evidence of their standing.

Maria's father offered one sheep, three jugs of wine and ten skeins of wool yarn as her dowry.

Petar responded, "*Kaj moras*—what can you do—must my eldest grandson be asked to marry a woman whose family does not respect her, and who show it by offering such a miserly dowry? Helena and I must think on this. But, surely, you will visit us next week, when you have had a chance to consider the matter further."

Maria knew the truth was that her parents, like all Kostelians, had little for themselves, much less a dowry.

Everyone was poor after paying taxes to the Lord of the Castle and tithes to the church on the many saints' days. To conclude the negotiations, her father finally added two piglets from next year's litter, and he agreed to pay for the large party following the wedding. That was his final offer, which sealed the contract.

Jerking awake, Maria looked down at Anton, as the youngster stirred and stretched but remained asleep. Helena sat beside her and looked at her sympathetically.

Startled to see the old woman, Maria asked, "Nana, I have been looking for you. Where have you been?"

"A group of the village elders has been discussing the situation and, as is usual, there are many opinions, but there are really few practical options. I am leaving for a short while and going with Petar and Steffan. We will see what the Turks are doing. Perhaps, the men will also burn the ferry."

"Oh, Nana, it will be dangerous."

"Yes, there is some danger, but there is no moonlight tonight, so our movements should go unnoticed. Sleep some more if you can, Maria. We will return soon."

"Oh, Nana . . ." Maria tried to continue, but the older woman slowly stood and shuffled toward the mouth of the cave.

CHAPTER FIVE

Steffan knew there was nothing the villagers could do to prevent the Turks from attacking in the morning. Perhaps they could persuade the attackers to avoid Kostel and continue downstream in their terrifying quest for young captives. His plan was to torch the ferry with his grandfather's help.

The river crossing was on a major, heavily used road and the ferry would need to be replaced quickly. Unfortunately, wheat-harvesting season neared in the next few weeks. Yet, destroying it was the only way to try to block them. Even then, he knew that the raiders might choose to swim their horses across the river; however, the Turkish wagons would have to remain on the opposite bank. Setting it ablaze might also delay the attackers until the castle soldiers arrived. Steffan considered that event to be hopeless, as more than sufficient time had already passed for their arrival.

The hamlet of Am Furtt sat more than a mile east and downstream from Brod na Kupi, which was located on the opposite riverbank. The main road between Adriatic ports in the southwest, such as Rijeka and Opatija, to Gottschee in the north, and even more distantly to Vienna, crossed the river using the Am Furtt ferry and toll crossing. Steffan knew some in Brod spoke of building a wooden or stone bridge over the river rapids at their location. Apparently, such talk had been going on for years and was more prevalent at the time the Zrinski Castle was completed twenty years earlier. No current plans were under consideration.

Further, the village of Market Kostel, located several additional miles east and downstream from Am Furtt, sat at the foot of an imposing rock outcropping with the castle sprawled over the hillside. Its location, like Brod, lacked a suitable place for a river crossing. The result was that the small hamlet of Am Furtt served a broad stretch of farming settlements and small towns on both sides of the Kupa River, besides being a major link on the main north-south road.

Petar had told Steffan that in years past there had been an unspoken agreement between the Klobucar family and marauding Turkish bands. The raiders needed a way to cross the waterway with their wagons, and Am Furtt villagers wanted to survive: As a result, the Turks operated the barge themselves, transporting their column of men and wagons, while the villagers remained hidden in the cave. When the raiders departed, a few stolen horses or cows remained at the crossing, as payment for the unspoken agreement. Of course, all the animals rightly belonged to Count Erdody, but Petar always kept one. He sold the animal in Brod and divided the money among village families.

The Turk's unsuccessful attack on Vienna and Gottschee in recent years had changed everything. During the army's southern return, the defeated Turks had been unusually brutal. They had tortured and viciously murdered several Kostelians. Later, the severed heads of the dead appeared on sharp stakes planted along the riverbank near the toll crossing. As a final act of mayhem, the Turks had cut the lines to the barge, allowing it to drift with the current and break up in the rapids downriver.

Villagers discussed the current dangerous situation earlier in the evening. Many offered opinions, but finally, burning the ferry was the only plan that seemed to have any chance of slowing the Turks. Petar was the mayor, so it fell to him and his son to set the fire. The two snuck back to their barn for casks of highly flammable solvent, a liquid distilled every fall from the resin of selected pine trees.

Where in the hell are those fighting men from the castle? Steffan wondered. *They have had plenty of time to travel here. They know this is the major crossing on the river, and any attackers will have to use it. I hope they are not sitting on their arses, as father suspects. Maybe the Turks have something else in mind besides harvesting Kostel. Perhaps, they will also scout a new trail to Gottschee. It would take a significant force to attack that much larger and prosperous town.*

"Hurry, Grandfather," Steffan whispered. "We must soak all the wood so that the barge will burn swiftly and be swept away by the current."

"I am coming, but my legs move slowly these days, and the cask is heavy." Petar also carried flint in his pocket and a sack of oil-soaked rags to ignite the solvent.

Steffan reached the barge first, carrying his barrel. He stepped aboard carefully and looked at the Turkish encampment, some fifty yards on the opposite side of the river. He saw guards patrolling along the riverbank and the faint shapes of wagons and pitched tents against the glow of low burning campfires.

The two finished emptying the casks, and Petar stooped to light the rags. He struck the iron piece on the flint to create a spark. Once, twice and then again, he struck one against the other, but each spark was weak while the sounds of the rushing river masked the sharp click.

Across the river, Steffan watched, as guards continued to patrol.

Petar tried again, with only a flash in the dark night for his effort. *"Drek*—shit," he swore.

Steffan observed one guard stopping and pointing across the river, apparently having seen the flash. He must have called out, as other guards hurried to the edge of the water.

"Grandfather, they saw the last spark!"

Grumbling, Petar struck the flint again. With that attempt, the rags ignited swiftly, causing the old man to pull back and stand quickly. He lost his balance and nearly fell into the river before Steffan steadied him.

Steffan looked across to the encampment, as a soldier leveled his musket. He saw the flash of a gun, followed by the sound of a lead musket ball whizzing past his head a moment later. The flames spread rapidly, following the trail of distilled spirits. In the light of the fire, the barge and both men were visible. *"Stari,"* Steffan called, using his pet name—old man—for his grandfather, "the soldiers will see us from the light of the fire. Hurry, we must return by way of the toll path."

He heard the whine of musket balls thudding into the wooden barge.

Suddenly, Petar fell. "Help me, son! I may have broken my ankle."

Steffan hoisted the man onto his back and tried to move swiftly, but the barge was unsteady.

"Ahh," his grandfather cried out. "They shot me in the arm."

Upon reaching the riverbank, Steffan staggered up the path, carrying his grandfather. There was more gunfire and then the sound of a lead ball striking, which knocked the two of them to the ground. Quickly checking himself, he felt no pain. "*Stari*, have you been shot again?" he shouted, his voice rising in desperation.

"*Stari*," his voice was frantic, cracking with emotion. "Answer me! Did they hit you again? Grandfather, speak to me! Please, say something!"

He rolled the old man over and explored the back of his grandfather's tunic in the last light from the burning craft. It was wet and red. There was no response from his grandfather.

His *Stari* would never speak again!

Helena watched Steffan carry Petar beyond the range of the Turkish gunfire, her husband's arms hanging down limply, as the two slowly made their way along the path, faintly silhouetted by the dying fire. Her fist flew to her lips, and she bit down hard on her knuckle to prevent herself from crying out.

The young man laid Petar on the dirt path in front of her, as he sobbed and his whole frame trembled with spasms of grief. "Why has this evil befallen us, Nana? Why must they murder my *Stari*? Why must the evil-doers always bring their terrible hatred for us, and torment our people?"

Helena knelt and reached over her husband to embrace her grandson. Tears rolled down her cheeks, as she gently rocked him. "I have no answer, son of my son. If this is God's will, then there is justice somewhere, but it is not here—not on this morning in this land of ours." She made the sign of the cross over Petar and recited, "May the Lord, Jesus Christ, protect you and lead you quickly through purgatory, allowing you to enter eternal life and to take your place beside our Lord."

Helena pulled back and stared at the young man in the dark while wiping away her tears with her shawl. She steeled herself and spoke softly. "Steffan, you now head the Klobucar family. The right to live and work the land now rests with you. The family burdens are on your shoulders."

"They killed him, Nana Helena," Steffan sobbed. "These bastards have tormented Christians like us for more years than we can count. Why do they do that, Nana? What drives them to such ungodly acts? Is it not against their beliefs, as it is against ours, that thou shall not kill? It is a tenant from our Lord—why, then, must we be the ones who suffer?"

"I have no answer," she responded gently. "You will have an opportunity to ask the priests, and they may find a reason. But, listen to me and listen well! These evil men will find a way to cross the river tomorrow. There is nothing more you or I can do."

Steffan looked at her, tears glistening in his eyes. "We must give *Stari* a Christian burial and have a feast, which will celebrate his life, and then we must have the priests pray for his soul. Those are our customs."

"His last confessional, thank God, was on Friday. Right now, you and I must think of the living. There will be time enough to mourn our loss later. We must leave your *Stari* here on the toll path. The Turks may find him and have their way, but he no longer feels any pain or fear. He is with our Lord."

"Nana, we cannot leave him. Those Turkish animals will mutilate his body. We must hide him. And he must have a proper burial with words spoken over him by the priests, to assist the passage of his immortal soul through purgatory, so that he can reach God's Kingdom."

"Listen to me, Steffan, we will pray for him every time we go to Sunday Mass and on All Souls' Day, on the second of November. Our efforts will help him move more quickly through purgatory and allow him to take his rightful place with the Lord. Then, your grandfather will be the same age as Jesus when he died, thirty-three, and in perfect health and condition. You know all this, so hear my next words well. We must consider other matters at this very moment. You have a wife and a son to think of, who are sitting in the cave. Our neighbors in the village are quaking in their sandals. There is no time for funerals or priests sprinkling holy water. If we leave him here, the raiders may think they have avenged the burning of the barge and will get on with their evil work. No! He must remain right here, and we must brush away our tracks. Come, and do as I say. The morning sunrise approaches!"

Standing, Steffan stared down at his *Stari* in the faint light, as the old man lay crumpled on the dirt path. Making the sign of the cross, he followed his grandmother to the orchard, and in the very last light from the burning toll boat, they used branches to sweep away their footprints.

Steffan bent his head in prayer and then made the sign of a cross.

Helena also bowed her head. *Oh Lord, I ask for deliverance from that which still may befall us this morning. God, please grant me this wish to keep my family and neighbors safe.* She opened her eyes, as her tears flowed freely again. Then, she made the sign and turned toward the forest.

CHAPTER SIX

The cave was eerily quiet. A draft chilled Maria, as she pulled her woolen shawl closer around her shoulders. The movement awakened Anton, who was hungry. Maria shifted her bodice and tunic and let him feed. With great difficulty, she calmed herself, and her thoughts returned to the Klobucar household and her marriage to Steffan, as a way to take her mind off their peril.

Helena was supportive and smoothed Maria's acceptance into the family from the beginning. Nana became her ally during times when the household became tense over various incidents. Maria was thankful for the older woman's understanding, patience and the fact that her approach differed so markedly from others in the fiefdom.

The marriage produced some uneasy feelings with Steffan's brothers and sisters. Custom dictated that all the children, except the eldest son, should eventually leave the family home and make their lives elsewhere unless the patriarch divided the hide's land among his sons. In Petar and Helena's opinion, smaller parcels was not a possibility, as these might be insufficient to support a family.

Some issues in the family resolved naturally, when Petar and Helena arranged marriages for Steffan's two sisters within the following months, as a Klobucar dowry accompanying the family's granddaughters was valued. The family was not wealthy. Still, their financial circumstances were better than most. They had the income from their share of the ferry and toll collections, in addition to their hide.

For his brothers, the question of surnames became a factor. Establishing family names in the early sixteenth century had been a significant societal occasion and a source of pride for serfs. Yet, there were no set rules for creating surnames. Some used the name of their village or a feature of the landscape. However, in the Klobucar case, it was more straightforward. In an earlier time, family ancestors had made hats and sold them widely throughout the empire, including at major shipping ports located along the Adriatic Sea. Locally, the word for "hat" was *klobuca*; this evolved into *Klobucar*.

Nearly all serfs were illiterate. Yet, if one brought a sweet treat to a parish priest, such as slices of cheese strudel, or better yet, a flagon of wine or a small jug of *rakia,* and asked nicely, the holy man might show the person the Church's original birth entry, recorded in the *Book of Births*. It was one of three separate volumes, containing chronological listings in the Catholic parish's records; collectively, they were the *Book of Souls*. The one for births listed the serf's name, baptism date, along with the names of parents and godparents, all written in Latin. For another slice of strudel, a serf might persuade the priest or novice to write their name on a piece of wood, which the person held as a treasured possession. It did not matter that the serf could not read and that he or she signed their name with an "X." Their surname belonged to them.

Steffan's two brothers took different routes in leaving their birth home. One married a widow, whose husband died when a tree blew down in the forest. The woman had four daughters, which left the "right to work the land" heritage in jeopardy. As a result, the widow, who was still of childbearing age, sought a husband. Although she was older by eight years, Steffan's brother looked forward to having his own farm, and thus, the widow became another Mrs. Klobucar in the village of Am Furtt.

The route of the second brother took a different turn, involving a surname of another family, which also had no sons. The young woman's father agreed to the marriage of his daughter if Steffan's brother changed his surname to Lissic, the bride's family name, assuring the continuance and legacy of that family. The debate was extensive in the Klobucar household, but in the end, his brother agreed to the arrangement. Both families made a point of going to the parish church to assure that a full recordation appeared in both the *Book of Souls,* in this instance the *Book of Marriages*, and in the *Status Animarum,* the priests' condensed records for the clergy's personal use.

In the dimly lit cave, these and other thoughts occupied Maria's mind, as the long wait for daylight continued. Somewhere in the large cave, a child cried out. A shiver of fear chilled her, and once more, she hugged her son to her breast.

CHAPTER SEVEN

Saint George's Day
Market Kostel
1694

Johannes scanned the crowd. The rhythmic strumming of the two-string gusle suddenly stopped, startling those absorbed in the tale. Others, who had been talking in soft voices, looked at him. The quiet of the stillness took on a measure of heaviness. He gently rocked himself, substituting rhythmic body motions for the sound of the instrument. From his robe, he produced his flask and drank deeply once more before continuing.

> "I heard long ago
> And in this way
> Tell all to know"

The crowd knew that tales of Turkish attacks always contained mayhem, as did the current one. From previous times, they also knew that the current story was about to take a turn for the worst, as it was a story of their ancestors. Indeed, the entire region had heard it many times. People never tired of hearing about the bravery, death and sacrifice contained in the tale. Rather, it captivated them, for it was a story of evil versus good, might against courage.

"Good people of Kostel," Johannes began once again, as his fingers found the strings, "at sunrise on the morning of the fire, Steffan and two others departed the cave and cautiously made their way back to the river's edge. They remained hidden in the tall reeds growing beside the riverbank. Carefully, they looked across the fast-moving water to the raiders' campsite, but there was no sign of the Turks or their camp. Not daring to believe that the plan had worked, the three men waited and listened for a considerable period until early morning light confirmed their observations. They stood and rushed back to the cave to report what they had seen with their spirits soaring.

"The Klobucars collected Petar's body with the help of other villagers and prepared it for burial. Life was gone, but the opportunity was real for Petar to reside in heaven. All of you know the Church's doctrine and, if I misspeak, I am sure that our clergy friends here today will correct me. Catholic teachings hold that the soul separates from the body at death, but in the resurrection, God provides everlasting life to the dead, transformed by a reunion with the soul. Just as Christ rose and lives forever, so all of us hope to do the same in the afterlife.

"But, first, souls must move through a state of punishment, where they suffer agony to atone for sins committed during life. Survivors of the deceased can reduce the length of time in purgatory for the dearly departed, as all of you know, by offering prayers, taking communion and performing acts of penance.

"Helena had already contemplated making such sacrifices, and she knew others in the family would follow her lead. She hoped Steffan might agree to wear a hair shirt, made of woven twigs and animal skin. The abrasiveness of the blouse rubbed and irritated the skin, adding another layer of significant contrition to his penance.

"At the cemetery, only the burial and blessing remained; and afterward, there would be a feast as tradition demanded." With an immense sigh, Johannes intoned, "Young Maria tried comforting Helena, as they walked arm-in-arm behind the slow-moving horse-drawn cart that carried the body of Petar Klobucar. The sad procession continued, but strangely, there was no sign of soldiers from the castle. As they passed other hamlets, more peasants joined, until the line behind the cart extended for a considerable distance.

"I am never certain how it occurs, but the news of Petar's death moved quickly throughout the fiefdom. Few had slept the previous night, and many had seen the glow in the dark sky from the burning ferry. More than one man carried a shovel for the digging that awaited them at the burial ground that day. Afterward, mourners would pass the grave, tossing flowers or handfuls of dirt into the pit. It was a way of showing respect and bringing closure.

"Wailing is our way to voice grief, a long-held custom that I suppose dates back to the beginning of mankind. Many mournful sounds filled the air that day and cast a mood of sorrow along the processional. Others spoke quietly to each other about the courage required to burn the barge. Petar's act was on the minds and lips of many that morning.

"Certainly, it was on the mind of Aga Abdul Azim, as the fire had upset his plans. As he had watched the flames consume the barge the night before, he had sworn vengeance."

CHAPTER EIGHT

Turkish Camp
Kupa River

Aga Abdul Azim was beside himself with rage. Waiting to cross the river until morning had been a mistake, and he felt it reflected poorly on his judgment in the eyes of the troop. He punched one fist hard into his other hand as he watched the flames consume the barge. With a quick, decisive move, he drew his *yatagan* and furiously hacked at the ferry's draw line in frustration, finally severing it. Then he turned and slashed the rope holding the iron triangle, which travelers struck with a hanging metal rod to call for ferry service from the other side of the river. Rarely had he lost his temper so completely before his men.

"What a setback," Tasar lamented. "Why does it have to happen now of all times—just as I was about to lose my celibacy?"

Snarling, Azim commanded, "Give the order to break camp at once. We are leaving. The castle garrison must have arrived and set the fire. I doubt that the villagers had enough daring to burn the ferry."

"But, Aga, our maps only show the lands adjacent to the river," his second in command commented. "We could lose our way in the forest at night, or possibly fall over a cliff."

"What have we to fear? Are we like the serfs waiting for us across the river? You think we should run like rabbits. You heard my order—now see to it at once, and have the slaves prepare enough torches to light our way! We will find another campsite. The most important thing right now is that we must depart this area quickly. Leave one man behind and have him remain concealed in the brush. Order him to report immediately on any activity he sees across the river. And, tell him, if he falls asleep, it will cost him his head!"

"Very well, it appears that you have a plan?"

"We will talk soon enough."

It took the party hours to travel several miles downriver, where they took shelter and made another camp in a glen behind a hillside, well removed from the water.

Holding a flaming torch and surveying the new site, Azim gave several orders in quick succession. "There are to be no cook fires tonight, Tasar. Douse all but a few of the torches, and tell the men to be quiet. There will be no unnecessary talking. Station men with the animals, to assure they remain calm. I do not want our location known across the river. Is that clear, Tasar?"

"Yes, my Aga."

"Then, assemble our Janissaries and bring the leader of the irregular Bosnian forces. We must talk about my plan to attack the castle."

His second officer raised an eyebrow, but with his commander in such an agitated state, he thought it best to say nothing and left to comply.

Shortly, Azim gathered the men around him, beneath the light cast by a single torch. He knelt and began drawing in the dirt with a stick. "This is the river," he said, drawing a line. "The ferry crossing and the village of Am Furtt are here," he said, making an "X" on the ground. "Downriver, this is the location of Kostel Castle," he continued, making another mark.

Looking at the leader of the men from Bosnia, he said, "Istani, choose your four best men. I want them to swim their horses across the river when we conclude this meeting. Have them dress as hermits. Send two to the Christian church. They will make preparations to set it ablaze when they hear the sound of the cannon."

Unsure, the rebel leader asked, "Whose cannon, Aga?"

"Ours, of course!" Azim replied in exasperation. "Beforehand, your other two men will knock on the castle gate and gain entrance. When inside, they have two tasks—kill the castle commandant and his top sergeant."

Surprised, the man looked dubious. "How, Aga, do you suggest they do that?"

"Use your head, man! Have them pose as serfs fleeing from us. They can tell the castle guards that they have news of our movements, and know about an attack we are planning after the changing of the guards in the morning. However, they are to say that they will only reveal the information to the commandant. From there, they can be creative. *Understand?*"

With some reluctance, the man nodded.

"At dawn, you and the remainder of your men will begin an attack on the castle."

Wide-eyed, the Bosnian stared at him in amazement. Finally finding his voice, he sputtered, "But, Aga, the castle has five defense towers plus stone walls that are six feet thick, which rise too tall for us to scale without special equipment. We can do little damage with our muskets and the portable cannon that we carry with us."

"You do not understand," Azim replied, impatiently. "Your group will stay on this side of the river to carry out the attack. The castle battlements are less than two hundred yards away and still within range of the arrows from our longbows, cannon and musket balls. You will fire exactly ten volleys. Between each, you will count to three hundred. Is that clear?"

"Attack with the small four-pound abus, Aga? It will do no real damage to the walls, much less breach them," the Muslim leader noted, looking for support from others circled around their commander. Hurriedly, he continued, "And, it is reported that the castle has several large cannons that can easily bombard our position."

Disdainfully, Azim continued, "Do not be idiotic, Istani, your attack is a trick. The job of you and your men is to deceive the soldiers in the castle. Between burning the church, losing their officers and your hail of fire, there will be much confusion on the other side. They will probably think that a large force is attacking them. That will keep their soldiers within the walls. Also, the reports from our spies indicate that their cannons cover the road that passes to the north of the castle. It will take time for them to respond and muscle those big guns to the southern battlements facing you across the river. By then, you and your men will have left the area and returned here."

"Yes, now I understand," the Bosnian leader replied, a smile replacing the frown on his face. "So, Aga, what about you and your Janissaries—what task will you perform?"

At that moment, the man left behind at the abandoned camp at the river approached Tasar and whispered to him.

His second in command hurried toward Azim and said, "Aga, our man believes the villagers may have set the toll barge on fire. He watched men scouting our camp from the opposite side of the river. None wore uniforms or armor. He says that they were dressed like serfs."

"Hmm, so these farmers want to play at war, do they?" Azim mused aloud. "I had more *devsirme* in mind, Istani, while your men kept the castle occupied. However, this news changes things. To answer your question, my Bosnian friend, the Janissaries will swim our horses across and return upriver. The peasants of Am Furtt have denied us the use of the ferry, and for that, they will pay dearly."

"It is a good plan, Aga," Tasar commented.

"And, let us not forget the young captives that we have harvested already," Azim continued. "Tasar, set our strongest black slaves to guard them. The children must remain safe until our return. Are there any questions?" Hearing no response, he quickly continued, "Good! Let us prepare for our tasks as the fullness of dawn approaches!"

CHAPTER NINE

Am Furtt

Men from the village carried Petar's body to the house to allow preparation for burial to begin. This included washing Petar and dressing him in his finest tunic.

Tears rolled down Maria's face, as she helped Helena. She fetched fresh water and watched Helena use a sharp knife to cut away his bloody tunic. Between them, they cleaned the body and dressed him in a white robe, rolling him over more than once to dress him in the fresh garment. Except for Steffan, she had never touched a grown man in that way. The musket wounds made Maria queasy. However, Helena showed no emotion, and her hands remained steady as the work continued.

Throughout the task, Steffan stood to one side, holding baby Anton and watched.

Maria saw the blaze of fury in his eyes behind his tears.

When Anton became restless, Steffan handed him to Maria, who turned aside and entered the bedroom. Releasing her breast, she fed the hungry child.

As their work ended, Helena instructed, "Son of my son, please hitch the cart and horse and make sure there is fresh straw in the bed. We will pray for your grandfather and bury him in the cemetery next to the church in Fara."

Drying his eyes and without saying a word, the young man left the house.

Both women dressed in black, from the babushkas on their heads to their leather sandals. By tradition, Helena would wear that color for the remainder of her life, both out of respect for her husband and as a sign of continued mourning, while donning black would end in one year for Maria.

Soon, everything was ready. The entire village of Am Furtt, except a crippled woman, fell in line behind the two women with everyone dressed in black. Maria knew well that a procession like this was far from unusual given the high number of deaths among children and the many trips to the graveyard. Some women wailed loudly to evidence their mournful grief.

Steffan and a village boy walked ahead leading the horse-pulled cart. The dirt road ran along the edges of pastures and fields of grain, generally following the bends of the river. As the procession passed other hamlets, more villagers, dressed in black, joined the line. In the bed of the wagon, Petar appeared to be resting peacefully, his gray hair neatly brushed, as though he was sleeping while on the way to Sunday church service.

There was a light breeze that morning, and it felt refreshing to Maria after spending the night in the damp cave. She wished she knew how to console Helena better, but the elderly woman gave every appearance of being in self-control, staring straight ahead. Nana Helena walked slowly and steadied herself by holding onto the cart. Her other hand held a black shawl closed at her neck.

Despite the long night and fitful bouts of sleep in the cave, helping Helena prepare Petar that morning left Maria unusually edgy. She whispered to Helena that she wanted to stretch her legs and lengthened her stride with Anton in her arms. Drawing abreast of Steffan, Maria glanced sideways, but his eyes remained fixed, straight ahead. Then, he was ten or twelve paces behind her.

Nearing the crest of a low rise, she heard the sound of hoof beats approaching from the other side. *It has to be soldiers from the castle,* she thought, *and they are searching for the Turks. It is about time! After all, that is part of the grand bargain of serfdom, is it not? We serfs work the land and pay the taxes while the fiefdom Lord protects us.*

Topping the rise, she stopped suddenly and then cried, "Oh, my God—it cannot be!"

There, like a wild horde of whirling dervishes, a small band of Janissary cavalry swiftly approached, their billowing robes flowing behind them in a bright cascade of color. Unsheathed *yatagan* blades flashed in the light of the bright morning sun.

At the same instant, Maria also noticed black smudges of smoke in the distant sky and heard the faint reports of muskets and cannon fire. A battle was apparently raging at the castle. Far from giving up their quest, the Turks had changed tactics.

A wave of fear gripped her. She stared a moment longer, her mouth open while Anton suckled her breast. Then, turning quickly, she shouted, *"EVERYONE, HEAR ME! STOP! THE TURKS ARE RIDING TOWARD US. RUN TO THE RIVER OR THE FOREST AND HIDE! THEIR SWORDS ARE*

ALREADY SWINGING AND HORSETAILS HANG FROM THE TOPS OF THEIR LANCES. FOR THE LOVE OF GOD, HURRY AND SAVE YOURSELF!"

There was a moment of startled confusion, and then Kostelians began dispersing, running through the fields of grain. The atmosphere became feverish as people inadvertently collided and children fell to the ground.

Looking down the procession from the knoll, it reminded Maria for a brief moment of the biblical story where Moses parted the Red Sea. People split away to each side of the road, as news of the advancing Turks traveled down the line of mourners. Shortly, only the boy tending the cart, Helena, Steffan and Maria with the baby stood on the road.

Running toward the cart in panic, Maria shouted, "Steffan, what should we do?"

Her husband did not answer, yet the blood had drained from his face. He pulled a small knife from a fold of his tunic. Everyone carried such a blade for eating. It appeared ridiculously puny, considering the flashing swords headed toward them.

Shocked at the turn of events, Steffan commanded, "Maria, take Anton and run to the drying shed on the far side of the field. Conceal yourselves there! Nana and I will stay here with *Stari*." To the boy, he said, "Milo, run into the tall grass thirty steps, then lie flat and, by all that is holy, stay still and do not move."

"I cannot leave you here by yourselves with those men coming," Maria replied. She was both defiant and frightened, as her son squirmed in her arms.

Approaching her in two quick steps, Steffan slapped her hard across the face. "Do as I say, woman! Think of our son! You must try to save yourselves. For Nana and me, what will be, will be. There is no time to argue. Now, run!"

With that, he gave her a firm shove in the direction of the shed.

    Nodding, and with tears glistening in her eyes, she hurried away, glancing over her shoulder once to see Steffan and Helena staring in the direction of the approaching riders.

CHAPTER TEN

Standing tall in his stirrups, Aga Azim saw the cart on the road and the people running through the fields on both sides of the road. "Tasar," he instructed, "take your men after the villagers. Sort out five children to take back with us, and bring everyone else to the road."

"Yes, my Aga." Wheeling his mount, he and his men were soon pursuing the serfs.

Abdul and one soldier continued toward the cart. A quick glance told him that the old woman and young man were related. "You," he said to his trooper, speaking in the native language of their youth.

"See that the head of the dead man is severed, and add it to our bag of trophies. Then, have his remains tossed into the river. This is obviously one of the serfs who burned the ferry last night and was killed by our men."

"No," the old woman shouted. "My husband was a good man and worked hard all of his life."

While her accent and dialect differed, he knew that the two of them understood each other.

Continuing, she said, "I beg you, let him rest in peace with his God, now that he is in heaven! Your men took his life. Is that not enough?"

"Shut up, old woman, and stay out of our way. Trooper, carry out my order!"

"You cannot do that!" the woman stormed. "Your order is godless," she shouted, leaving the wagon and charging at him and his horse on frail legs. "I will not let you, I tell you! You will not mutilate my husband!"

Without hesitation, Azim brought the hilt of his sword down, knocking the old woman unconscious.

Seeing movement out of the corner of his eye, he quickly wheeled his horse about, until the tip of his curved sword pricked the skin of the younger man. "Hold fast, you damned fool," he commanded, again in the language of that region. "This woman will be all right. I assume the dead man in the cart is a relative." Without waiting for a reply, he continued, "You and this old woman have already lost a member of your family. Who will head your household, if you challenge me and lose your life doing something stupid with that little eating knife?"

Azim's words stopped the young man, who stared at him with rage burning in his eyes. Slowly, he lowered his gaze and dropped the knife.

To his trooper, Azim commanded, "Tie this one to the wagon and give him ten lashes of the whip. We will let him live for another day."

Quickly looking afield, he saw Tasar's men beginning to herd the villagers toward the road, as his second approached. "You, Tasar, make sure the serfs are secure and that the young captives you selected begin marching back to the place where we swam the river. Give ten lashes to every third man and burn every second drying shed along this stretch of the river. Then, if it pleases the men, all of them can have their way with the women. However, hear me good, let the old ones and the rest of the children flee—there will be no killing, Tasar, unless your men meet resistance. Better to instill fear into the hearts of these serfs, while allowing them to breed again, so our future harvests of young ones continue to be plentiful. Are my orders understood?"

"Yes, my Aga."

"This should teach the Kostelians a useful lesson for the future. It is folly for them to resist the advances of Janissaries."

"Yes, there is wisdom in what you say, Aga."

Scanning the surrounding fields, he saw a dark-haired woman running on the far side of the field. He touched his spurs to the flanks of the horse, and the nimble animal was after her in an instant.

Maria briefly turned her head again to look back at Steffan and Helena, then continued to hurry, seeking a hiding place in the storage shed ahead. It was awkward to run holding Anton in her arms, yet she continued. She heard the pounding hoof beats of a horse, which told her that the Turk had seen her and that she was being pursued. *Just a few more yards and I will set Anton down and arm myself with a hayfork from the shed,* she thought, grimly.

As the horse and rider closed on her, she cut sharply to the right at the last moment and ducked beneath the man's outstretched hand as he rode by and grasped the babushka off her head. The rider wheeled to the right, but Maria had already reversed course and was running to the left toward the door of the shed. She had nearly reached it when the man leaped from the saddle of his horse and brought her down.

The two plus Anton tumbled in the field until she quickly leaped to her feet and scooped up her son, looking at him anxiously and then hugged the boy to her bosom. "Let me be!" Maria shouted, her face flushed with fury and standing her ground. "Are you trying to kill my son and me?" Her fear had given way to anger for her son. "Heathens like you have no concern for anything. Leave my son and me alone, you devil-man from hell!"

While hurrying through the fields, her long hair had partially tumbled down, and the Turk grabbed a fistful and held her at arm's length.

Maria pulled her eating knife from her tunic and wildly lashed out, emitting a scream of terror.

The man nearly failed to react fast enough. Agile as a mountain cat, he moved outside her swing, and the blade missed, but it stabbed his horse in the buttocks. The startled animal immediately reared up on its hind legs and, despite its fine-honed training, galloped off with the sharp blade stuck in its rump.

"So, here we have a wildcat, eh?" the man noted with a grin, as he continued to hold Maria by her dark hair at arm's length. She struggled, but against the man's strength and size, there was little she could do.

"My name is Aga Abdul Azim, and I am the leader of the Muslim raiders."

"May you rot in hell, Aga Abdul Azim," she stormed, holding tightly to Anton. With a quick move, she kicked him in the leg and shouted, "You are a son of Satan, and you will burn in hell one day for the evil you bring to this land. Let go of me and my baby!"

Staring at him, there was no mistaking the lascivious look in the man's eyes as he stared at her heaving bosom. Maria shuddered as she briefly recalled the questions that had crossed her mind earlier that morning in the cave about the possibility of Turk's capturing her. *Is this when I am thrown to the ground and treated like a common prostitute,* she wondered. *Or even slaughtered? And what becomes of Anton?* A tremor prickled the hair on the back of her neck and tears filled her eyes.

Azim noticed the delicate features of the woman's face, as her light blue eyes flashed with rage and dread. His long-restrained passions stirred, as he stared at the lovely young woman struggling in his grasp. He also found that the rough and tumble capture heightened his sense of excitement.

He threw open the large door to the shed and dragged her into the darkened interior while the woman clutched the baby against her body. Then, he slammed the door shut behind them. Stepping into the middle of the shed, he hurriedly looked around the interior, his pulse quickening with anticipation, as he shaded his eyes against the strong glint of sunlight streaming in between the slatted sidewalls.

Smooth tree trunks, set in the ground at the corners and along the building's midsections, supported the double-storied building. Smaller timbers topped it above to form the roof and finish the basic structure. Thinner, horizontally placed wood created the sidewalls, each spaced about a hand-width apart, allowing air to flow through to dry cut hay and grasses. The building was partially full, as the distinct fragrance of sweet-smelling, cut fodder wafted through the humid air of the interior. From upper attic rafters, bundles of turnip greens, carrot tops, dandelions and assorted other vegetation hung down, dangling on long strings. These were also drying as feed for the family's pigs during the winter months.

The woman continued to kick and scream, weeping uncontrollably and fighting his attempts to calm her.

Using his handhold of her hair, he quickly swung her around.

Losing her footing, she stumbled and fell in the hay, as her black tunic flew up. Still angry, the young woman rose to her feet quickly, never releasing her hold on the baby. Staring defiantly, she shouted, "Leave us alone, you Turkish mongrel."

With quick movements, Azim moved close to the woman and then shoved her back, briefly diverting her attention, and snatched the baby from her grasp.

The woman let out a wildcat scream. "What are you doing?" she yelled, rushing at him and raking her clawed fingernails down the side of his cheek. "Give my baby back to me!"

Slapping her across the face smartly, Azim stepped back and gingerly ran his fingers over the scratches. Terrifyingly, he smiled at her while shifting the baby in his arms. As the child's wrap fell away, he noticed that it was a boy.

Wide-eyed and confused, the woman stopped crying. Her blue eyes turned dark, filled with apprehension for her son.

"Yes, a wildcat you are and the better it is. Now, listen carefully, for I will say this only once." With that, he raised the child high and turned him upside-down, holding the boy by his two legs with one hand.

Startled, the youngster let out a fearful cry.

The young mother stopped in mid-step. Her face became white with fear, and her hands trembled uncontrollably. "Stop! You are hurting him."

"He is fine, just a little confused, that is all," Azim answered. "What is your name, woman?"

She looked at him blankly.

The baby's screaming became raucous. Raising his voice, he said, "Do not play with me. With a quick swing, I can smash this baby's head against the side of the barn in an instant, and that will be the end of him. Is that what you want? Now, answer me! How do they call you?"

Straightening and holding his gaze, she softly replied, "Maria—Maria Klobucar. Please, I beg you, do not hurt my son."

"Are you related to the dead man in the horse drawn cart?"

"Do not hurt my child."

"Answer me, woman!" he snapped, his temper flaring with impatience.

"Yes ... he is ... he was my husband's grandfather and the patriarch of the family farm. Why will you people not let us live in peace? We have done you no harm."

"You and the others have delayed my trip by at least two days, and more than likely, some of my men will be injured because of it. Nevertheless, that is no concern of yours. I have enough men with my half-dozen Janissary soldiers, the retinue of slaves and attendants to keep things tidy plus some twenty wily Bosnian brigands, to strike fear into the hearts of you and all the other people in this fiefdom."

The young woman stared at him oddly, unsure how the information related to her and her son.

"I was once your kind—born to Christian parents." Azim continued, hesitantly, searching for the right words. His tone became more subdued as the explanation continued. "I was taken from my village as a young boy, many years ago, and became a Janissary warrior. Now, I command my troop as an aga—a commander. Do you have any idea what that means? Do you realize the work, training, honor and responsibility that rest on my shoulders, vested in me by the leaders of the most civilized empire in the world?"

Maria hesitated, and then tersely asked, "Why do you speak in riddles? I have no desire to know your army rank, and how you live your life has no interest to me. But, I beg you—stop holding my son in that way."

Azim complied, shifting the child upright, and holding him in the crook of his arm. Immediately, the boy quieted.

"Thank you," she said. "You were probably torn from your family as a child. The storytellers recite terrible tales about men like you, your Ottoman Sultan and the people you call civilized. For the love of God, I beg an answer to one question. What becomes of the abducted children?"

In a softer tone, he answered, "The half-dozen Turks in my troop and I are part of an elite corps of the vast Turkish army. On any battlefield, we, the Janissaries, are the best trained and the greatest warriors. That is because we live by strict rules of discipline. Our corps alone numbers some thirty thousand."

"There are thousands of you?" Maria repeated, an astonished expression on her face. "And all of you were Christian-born children at one time?"

"Yes, that is correct for the most part. But that is not all—the total for all white captives—warriors, scholars, officials and servants—is over three times that figure."

"Oh, my God in heaven above," Maria said, clearly stunned. "I cannot believe it! Tens of thousands and triple that in total . . ." The young woman's eyes seemed to glaze over. "I cannot picture so many kidnapped children in my mind. Such a number must be as vast as the sheaves of wheat growing in our fields. I had no idea you Turks had taken your barbaric practices to such an unimaginable level. Why do you do these evil deeds? What is behind the cruelty of so many abductions that leave parents and villages brokenhearted?"

"Years ago, a Sultan set out to establish a new social order and a unique group of people within the Ottoman Empire. After so many years, it exists today. Quite simply, Maria, the white slaves who entered the Empire are unwaveringly loyal to our Sultan and more dependable than even court nobles or tribal leaders. We have become the backbone of the country, as we are its administrators and the elite units called upon during wartime."

She stared at him, as tears filled her eyes and ran down her cheeks. "What misery you and your kind have spread over Christian lands, to mothers and fathers and kin—to your own family—who lose their children and never see them again."

"You simply do not understand," Azim replied coldly. "The young ones have a chance for a better and fuller life with us than they could have ever achieved in a backwater fief like Kostel."

Maria was white-faced, as she stared at him. Seeming to regain her self-composure, she asked, "Why tell me all these things. I have no wish to know the evil ways of your life. And, what does any of this have to do with my son and me?"

Confusion was evident on the attractive woman's face. Still, he hesitated. *She has heard tales of past attacks from her own storytellers*, he decided, *so she has no illusions about what occurs next*. Even so, he remained hesitant and unsure how to proceed, hiding his disquiet by continuing to talk about his life as a soldier. "Do you know anything about the Janissaries?" he asked.

She shook her head, watching the boy in his arms. The befuddled expression on her face continued.

"All of us have benefited from being educated. For instance, most of us speak several languages—perhaps Arabic or Persian in addition to our birth language and Turkish. Those who are warriors are also versed in geography and mathematics, and we know some of the finer points of the arts and sciences. Of course, we are trained in weaponry and drilled for battle."

"So what? I am a poor serf, living a simple life in a small farming village in the Fiefdom of Kostel. All of your information is useless to me. Why do you continue talking about geography, whatever that is, and your superior training to murder people? If you are trying to impress me with the learning stuffed between the ears of your over-inflated head, you have come to the wrong person and at the worst time. A respected elder in my family and village died because your men killed him."

"A casualty of a greater conflict, I fear, Maria. Still, I am trying to be patient with you, answering your questions and explaining our way of life."

"None of your accomplishments mean anything to me. In fact, I will always think of you and your people as un-Christian heathens!"

He ignored her attempt to irritate him. "I have no reason to impress a plain and simple woman, such as you. All you know is milking cows, baking bread and delivering babies."

"Ha!" Maria stormed. Changing the subject, she asked, "What has happened to the man and woman who were with the cart and all the other villagers?"

"They should all be alive, as those were my orders."

"Praise God for that," she said, as she made a sign of the cross and placed her lips on the tip of her thumb. "Still, your men killed the man lying in the horse cart, who was the mayor of Am Furtt. Look at you, strutting your extensive training and knowledge, yet you were once just like us. How twisted your masters have made you!"

Trying to form his thoughts, Azim paid no attention to her ridicule. Instead, he stated the one matter that was uppermost in his mind. "And, all of us have practiced . . . strict self-denial."

"Do you know how stupid your words sound?" Despite the vulnerability of her position, the woman laughed scornfully, placed her hands on her hips and mocked him. "What does self-denial mean, and what does it have to do with my son and me? I have heard silly, half-wits make more sense than you do, as you ramble on about languages, Janissaries and your life as a Turk."

Suddenly more agitated and uneasy, Azim went on in a rush, "We are not permitted to grow facial hair. Further, we are celibate coteries," he finished, blushing, as sweat trickled down his back beneath his caftan in the shed's humid interior.

Bewildered, she responded, "You are clean shaven! How in the name of sanity does that have anything to do with my son and me? As to the rest of your fancy words, they are gibberish and make no sense to me. Were you not taught by your Turkish slave masters how to speak plainly?"

"All right," he said, pausing for only a moment, "none of us has copulated with a woman."

The befuddled expression on the pretty young woman's face told him that she still did not understand him.

Exasperated, he blurted, "Why the hell do you not grasp what I am repeatedly saying? Damn it, woman, there has been a rule against intimate relationships with females. Janissary white slaves may not lay with a woman and have sex. Is that plain enough for you?"

She stared at him in amazement, then her face reddened, as she finally understood his meaning. Her Catholic priests abstained from sexual acts with women, but it was evident that she was struggling with the idea that the same might be true for this man and his cadre of fellow warriors.

"Prohibiting female intimacy has been strictly enforced!" he continued, self-consciously, flushing and reddening with embarrassment. A nerve twitched in his cheek, and he repeatedly touched it with a finger. *Damn, I just need to say the words,* he thought. *I need to stop this dithering.* Drawing himself up in a dignified manner, one hand holding the baby and the other on the hilt of the *yatagan*, he added, "And we observe it with adherence to discipline. Even so, all males need to relieve their manly urges."

She watched him warily. Still, his words left her frightened. Less sure of herself, she remarked, "Your words continue to go around in a circle, yet they lead to no end and no beginning."

"You live in a farming hamlet and know the truth of my words. The nature of manhood requires an outlet. We Janissaries use boys, or other men, for that purpose—at least until now. My brethren and I have enforced that rule for centuries. That is how strict our discipline has been!"

The girl's face registered a look of astonishment, and he quickly concluded that the young woman had never considered unions between males.

Maria started to utter a comment, but glancing at her son, she bit her lip. Staring at him with wide-open eyes, she said, "I can understand that talking about such personal matters must make you uneasy. Again, I ask, what does any of this have to do with my son and me?"

"Recently, the rule about intimacy with women has changed..." He paused and flushed an even deeper shade of red.

"And—go on, get it out," she prompted.

"I stand before you as one who has never known a woman. This morning, in this shed, you will satisfy me as only a woman can. And, you will do so completely and willingly."

Astonished, Maria was speechless at his bold disrespect and gaped at him.

Anton, still resting on Azim's arm, began to squirm.

The young woman looked about with a wild, bewildered expression on her face, seeking a means of escape, but there was none. Then, her eyes moved to her son, and her face lost its high flush. Squarely facing him, she hesitated, then seemed to wilt before his gaze and offered a brief nod. "From the moment I saw you riding across the field, I knew what my fate might be today. Before anything else happens, please let me feed by son. It will calm him."

Azim nodded, and he handed the boy to her.

The woman adjusted her clothes, allowing the boy to nuzzle her. The baby stopped crying and suckled greedily. In a short time, he was fast asleep. Gently, Maria spread the baby's covering on a mat of soft grass and laid him down. Slowly turning, she looked at Azim with loathing. Her breathing was quick, and one leg trembled uncontrollably beneath her tunic.

CHAPTER ELEVEN

He motioned with his hand for her to move toward the center of the shed and to stand in a spot highlighted by a shaft of sunlight. When she did not move immediately, he again motioned her forward, scowling at her.

Timidly, she complied.

"Begin, please, by untangling your hair and running your fingers through it. I want to see its length."

Undoing the knot in her hair, it tumbled down, falling nearly to her waist.

"Now, take off your bodice and then your tunic. And, do it slowly!"

Lifting her head, Maria made no movement.

"Maybe," he said cruelly, "I should pick the boy up by his legs again and see if that will encourage you to be more cooperative."

"NO!"

"All right, begin disrobing by removing your bodice!" He felt the blood coursing through his body and the hot flush on his face. His arousal was already complete.

Slowly, Maria's fingers moved from one tie string to the next, until she was able to remove the black garment with a shrug of her shoulders.

"Now, take off your black tunic!"

Staring at her captor, Maria slipped the middle opening of the garment over her head and let it drop to the ground.

"And the undertunic next," Azim commanded.

"Please let my son live," Maria pleaded. "Promise me that."

"I am Janissary! You are my captive, and so is your son. Do as I command, or he will face the punishment you bring to him. Your undertunic—remove it!" he said, his breath wheezing in his dry throat from the exhilaration of having this beautiful woman under his control.

"No," Maria said, her voice quivering, but determined. "You must promise me first that no harm will come to my son?"

"How old is the boy?"

"Four months."

"How many male children do you have, Maria?"

"Only one, Anton."

"Then, yes, I can promise you that no harm will come to your first-born male. Even so, let my meaning be clear to you. As a woman, you will please me in every way. Anything I ask, you will do it willingly. Is that understood?" he asked.

She stared at him.

The expression on his face was resolute, yet tingling surges of anticipation and excitement ran through him, and the pace of his breathing increased. In fact, he felt as though his whole body was on fire, and his firmness boldly pushed against his caftan.

Lowering her eyes, she again nodded, looking sideways at her sleeping son.

"I did not hear your answer. Say it loud enough, so that even Allah can hear you."

Dismally, she answered, "Yes, I . . . understand what you ask. If I have your promise that my son will be unharmed and live, I will do as you ask."

"Very well, continue by removing the undertunic," he commanded.

She wavered, her face a mask of tormented self-consciousness and embarrassment. Slowly, she raised and slipped the long garment over her head. At first, it veiled her, then, despairingly and with tears of humiliation streaming down her face, she let the garment slip to the ground. She was naked, except for her woman's belt. Pulling it around, she untied the knot and it, too, fell to the ground.

"Stand right here," Azim demanded, pointing to a shaft of sunlight that streamed through a seam in the sidewall of the shed.

Stepping into the bright beam, Maria tried to cover her most intimate parts by using her hands and watched him, her blue eyes wild with fear. She glanced once at her sleeping son lying peacefully near the side of the shed, and then her shoulders dropped in resigned submissiveness.

He stood, totally mesmerized. Each breast was a handful, crowned by a distended nipple from the baby's feeding. Her hips flared, leading to a triangular thicket of dark curls above tapering legs.

Raising his hand, he motioned for her to turn around, fascinated by every curve of her womanly figure.

Blushing acutely, and tortured by her shameful exhibition, she reluctantly complied.

"You seem to have little extra weight remaining from the birth of your son," he observed.

"Milking cows, making bread and tilling the land with a baby strapped to my back tends to do that," she snapped.

Azim's mind flashed back to the Christian village, where he had been born. He had been happy there, until his kidnapping as a white slave. It took a long time for his terror and lonesomeness to diminish. Adapting, Azim learned to enjoy his new surroundings and way of life. Even so, he could still recall the warm smells of fresh bread his mother made, the special sweets that she saved only for him and his feeling of safety in her arms. Unexpectedly, Maria and her son had rekindled such memories . . . ones that for so long had remained buried.

"Once more, turn again," he commanded, circling his hand above his head.

The woman closed her eyes, appearing even more mortified, if possible, by his fixated examination. Her vulnerability and humiliation were utterly complete.

Azim took off his tall white hat, blouse, belt and flowing caftan, then his soft, leather boots. Hanging on one sidewall were large linen tarps, used to transport bundled hay from the fields to the shed. He took one down and laid it on the cut fodder, which formed a soft yielding pallet. He bent and easily lifted Maria in his arms, feeling her trembling warmth as he held her close against his chest. He carried her to the cloth and gently sat her down. Removing his genital support, he was thoroughly aroused.

"What is it you wish . . . from me?" Maria asked timidly, her voice dispirited, as she avoided looking at his nakedness.

Her question stopped him, as he stared at her. Lifting her chin with his hand, he looked into the depth of her startling blue eyes. Blushing and smiling thinly, he stammered, "I have already shamed myself by saying too much. You know that I have never lain with a woman. I ask . . . that you guide and teach me," he answered, lying on the pallet beside her, his breath whistling in his throat.

An astonished expression appeared on Maria's pretty face. It was plain to him that she had never taken the lead in such matters with her husband, and likely, with no one else. If possible, she seemed more nervous and distraught. Furtively, she glanced at her son, then toward the man at her side. "What do they call you?"

"I go by Azim, Aga Abdul Azim," he replied, lightly running his finger over her nipple.

She brushed his hand aside roughly. "No, I want to know your Christian name? Even you had one when you were born. What is it?" she demanded.

Flushing, he closed his eyes, and then replied, "Mathias."

"Lay here, Mathias."

CHAPTER TWELVE

Gradually, Maria roused herself from the depths of a mental haze. Through half-closed eyes, she languidly noticed the shed's rafters high above her. To the left, bright streaks decorated parts of the shed's interior, painted by dazzling rays of sunlight filtering in through the slatted sidewalls. There was an absence of reality in her state of lethargy. The slight flow of air through the openings was welcome and carried the fresh fragrance of grasses growing in the fields.

Suddenly, a warm body stirred next to her.

Instantly, Maria's eyes flew open, as a wave of memories washed over her, reminding her of the sinful acts she had committed with the Turkish soldier. Shocked to her very core, the bile of bitter revulsion suddenly stuck in the back of her throat, and a cloak of guilt overpowered her.

Guiding the Turk as he had commanded, Maria initially distanced herself emotionally from Mathias, remaining cold and unresponsive. She was in full control of her feelings, rigidly stiff and unyielding, her eyes fixed on the ceiling rafters. Quickly drained by his first effort, Mathias rolled onto his side and began kissing and caressing her gently, tracing light-touched patterns on her skin, as his fingers moved from one breast to the other. She tried—with all her moral and physical strength—to fix her mind on something else— anything that blotted out the awful situation forced upon her—as the man repeatedly fondled her tender breasts until they became taut. Then, he began teasing other intimate and sensitive areas.

Lying on her back, eyes closed tightly, breathing heavily and head spinning, Maria's desires and emotions climbed wildly. Slowly . . . involuntarily . . . her pent up needs as a woman ascended to unexplored heights, soaring unconsciously toward a level of fulfillment that was more complete than anything she had ever previously experienced. His stimulating caresses gradually blotted out her fears, anxieties and inhibitions—all swept away by the surging river of passion he ignited. In the end, she willingly responded to Mathias, voluntarily opening her thighs, raking his back with her fingernails and delighting in his kisses. When at last they lay exhausted, both dropped into a hazy land beyond wakefulness, mentally wallowing in the pleasurable depths of sated indulgence.

Lifting her head, she saw the Turk's hand resting on her breast. Livid at this utter sign of disrespect for her feelings, she threw it off furiously and moved her leg, breaking the light bond of intermingled sweat that joined them along their close-fitted bodies.

A dark shroud of shame engulfed her and overwhelmed her ability to think clearly. Maria suddenly gasped for air and quickly sat up, instantly feeling disoriented and nauseous. She glanced at Mathias, nude and resting on his back, with his eyes closed. The depth of her humiliation was complete, as she quickly looked away.

Her movements stirred him, and for long moments, he lay staring up at her. His dark, damp hair covered his brow in disheveled curls, and his brown eyes blinked drowsily. Getting to his knees and standing slowly, he took in the full measure of her figure, as she sat on the soft pallet, stark naked, overflowing with his fresh seed.

Maria looked away, horrified, and reached for her undertunic, slipping it over her head.

The man smiled knowingly at her, an expression of drained satisfaction on his face.

Quickly standing, Maria let the garment fall to cover her body, hiding her nakedness from the man's unwavering gaze. Quickly, she donned the rest of her clothes.

The Turk made no move to dress and stood brazenly naked, watching her. He reached out a hand to brush away bits of straw clinging to her clothes.

Roughly, she slapped it aside.

"You are my first, dear Maria, as you know. I will always remember this time."

The Turkish pig is obviously satisfied with himself, she thought. *He has no sympathy nor knowledge of the cruelty he brings.*

"You were gentle and kind," Azim continued. "And yet," he paused, "I know my passion moved you. All of this is new to me, still I felt you straining beneath me, breathing hard and clawing at my back with your fingernails!"

She could not bear to look at him. Instead, she hung her head and large tears fell from her eyes.

He moved closer to take her in his arms, apparently seeking to console her.

Maria stepped back and slapped his face angrily, retreating quickly. Her back was ramrod straight, and her expression was one of unmistakable loathing. Shrilly, she said, "Mathias, you whoremaster, smug self-satisfaction is written on your face, like a child who has stolen a ripe peach from his father's orchard and has not been caught. Finally, you have spilled your seed in a woman."

"And to you, my dear, I owe thee thanks," he murmured, his tone sincere.

Tersely, she added, "You were like a stumbling lamb seeking his mother's teat. And Maria from Am Furtt, a dumb unschooled serf took you in and fulfilled your wish to become a man, because you threatened to kill my only son." Her voice was scornfully frosty, "Yet, with neither remorse nor further thought, you savaged and raped me."

"Simply one of the spoils of victory, my dear," he grunted jauntily, his overbearing arrogance displayed crudely.

Angrily, she stormed, "Now, your self-esteem knows no bounds. You likely consider yourself a buck with a full rack or even, perhaps, the leader of a wolf pack. You stand naked before me, like the day your mother delivered you, with no modesty or shame—and obviously no concern for my feelings."

Frowning, the man stared at her. Then, he raised one eyebrow knowingly, smiled and moved his hand dismissively. "In the heat of our fiery passion, I moved you, did I not? I knew it then, and I see it in your eyes now. That is the reason why you are so angry. You are just as upset with yourself as you are with me. Oh, it did not happen during the first time. No, and it may not have been the second . . . at least, not at the beginning . . ."

Maria's face contorted into a mask of fury as she interrupted him. "You speak like a simpleton—a child caught up in a fantasy! Only the ass-end of a donkey would think such thoughts and then gloat about it," she stormed, springing at him, white-lipped and shaking with rage, as she sought to claw his eyes.

The Turk caught the flying fists, twisted her arms behind her back and powerfully lifted her off the ground.

Surprised by his strength, she raised her right knee quickly, aiming for his genitals.

He turned slightly and caught the knee on his thigh. "Where did a nice girl raised on a farm learn a ruse like that?" he asked. Holding both wrists in one hand, he bent her over, seeking to kiss her while fondling her breasts beneath the black tunic with his free hand.

In exasperation and with all her strength, Maria came down hard with both feet on the toes of his left foot. "You bastard, may you burn in the infernos of hell for all the misery you cause."

He released her, howling in pain, and darted about the shed on one leg. Then limping slightly and staring at her, he once again smiled and continued, "But, by the time we finished, your body moved with me, and you trembled in my arms. I know passion overcame you. By all that is holy, the third time was bliss for me, especially when I gently caressed you and you opened yourself to me. That is why you curse me now. In truth, your anger is with yourself, for responding like a woman, one who has lustful needs. Am I right? Surely, as a married woman, such feelings are not new to you?"

"*Drek*," she snarled, bitter and frustrated with outrage.

Watching her, his eyes narrowed, and he continued, "Maybe I am wrong? Am I the first to truly satisfy you, Maria?" With a thin, knowing smile, he continued, "I hope so and all the better, my dear, as that means we each shared something new with the other. You called me a stumbling lamb. Maybe those words are correct. I now know something else, though. I thrilled you today, and your body answered me—answered Aga Abdul Azim—the leader of the Turkish brigade. And, though you deny it, I moved you more than ever before, as our bodies came together as one."

"You are completely mad, and your ranting proves it! Does your conceit have no bounds of reason?"

"Ha, you entwined me, and for a moment, yes, my little serf wench, I did go out of my head with happiness at the joy of being a man. My back smarts where you raked me with your fingernails. That, my dear Maria, was you—expressing your passion, as we were both finally fulfilled."

"Your head swells like a sheepskin flagon full of water!"

"Why can you not be honest with yourself, Maria, and admit that I stirred you to new heights of delightful passion? We were in rhythm, the third time. We came together as lion and lioness, our bodies scorched in the white heat of the moment. You were the untamed lioness, straining beneath me, and I buried myself in you and roared like the black-maned leader of the pride."

Stunned, Maria stared at him, mortified at his description. "You are a cruel and violent man, paid to ravish Christians and, under the guise of your Sultan and religion, you steal our wealth—our little ones."

"Ha!"

"Our children are raised with motherly and fatherly love. You painfully separate child tributes from their parents and their God and then train them to become barbarians so they can kill their own people, just as you do. You seem supremely uncaring that converting the young ones to Islam leads to eternal damnation for Catholics—which is your fate also, Mathias. When you die, I cannot see your sins ever being forgotten or forgiven by my merciful Lord, for they obviously are too numerous and hideous to allow you passage through purgatory. As for me, you have jeopardized my immortal soul from ever sitting next to my Lord when my time comes in the afterlife."

"That is enough! I need no recital of catechism lessons from some inferior female serf whom I found running in the fields. There is no God but Allah, and Muhammad is

His only Prophet. You would know this if you had a proper education."

"You are just as evil as the devil's serpent in the Garden of Eden. Now you have tasted the forbidden fruit. That means darkness and hell await you, too, where you and your kind can reside with all the rest of the evil demons. All of you are demented, just like the religion you adhere to."

Insulted to the quick, he stormed, "You will not speak such blasphemy to me, you wretched woman. I do not need you, or anyone, to tell me who I am—a Janissary warrior, toiling for my Sultan. Still, you are right—you are a dim-witted serf, slave to the land you farm, who has little understanding of empires or anything else, other than what your priests read to you from their foolish Bible."

"Stealing is wrong in every society, and when it involves a woman's body, it is rape, Mathias. Our fiefdom banishes such an offender forever after he is relieved of his seed bag. If your empire has any decency at all, surely it holds the same view."

He only stared at her, ignoring her comment. "I could easily take you back to Istanbul with me as my slave, to do with as I command. There, you would pamper my every wish in exchange for the delights that I bestowed on you. The Qur'an and the sayings of the true Prophet, Muhammad, permit bondage for those who believe in other religions—for they are nonbelievers, such as you Catholics—according to our holy men of wisdom. Therefore, within Islam, an owner of a female slave, who is a nonbeliever, may enjoy her sexual favors. It raises the slave's status to that of a free wife and gives her standing before her master. When the girl becomes pregnant and bears his child, she is a free person after the death of her master. That seems to me to be quite fair to the maiden. Do you not agree?"

Still raging, Maria looked at the Turk contemptuously. "So, let me see if I understand this, because, as you have said, I am a mere serf of limited knowledge. Slavery is prohibited by your holy book and a holy man . . ."

". . . Muhammad, the one and only true Prophet."

". . . so, slavery is prohibited by holy laws, as established by your religion," she restated, "unless it is inconvenient to the needs or desires of your Sultan and Turkish nobles. I presume all of them are men. Is that right?" Not waiting for an answer, she rushed on, "And around this convoluted, upside-down interpretation, men are allowed to rape and demand sexual acts from slave women who are nonbelievers—despite rules prohibiting slavery in your religious book and the sayings of Mohammad. Do I have that right?"

For a moment, Azim seemed startled at hearing the logic of his words turned against him.

She continued, "All your gibberish is a pile of *drek* and Ottoman nonsense. Nevertheless, I do admit that I was wrong. I did not understand, until this moment, that your religion is not twisted and evil. Rather, it is the people practicing it—selfish barbarians like you, your men and your masters. If you do believe that slavery is good for some and bad for others, you are a simpleton with no decent or moral foundation. Why in heaven's name do you not think for yourself and see the glaring inconsistency? How can you go on denying the significant discrepancy between the words in your holy book and the misinterpretations by those who call themselves holy men?"

His eyes blazed. "That is enough of your loose words! Little do you know about Islam, for it draws on, and completes both Judaism and Christianity. It, dear Maria, is the *true* religion!"

Heatedly, she stormed, "Again, you speak muddled words and, most likely, these come to you from your

Ottoman slave masters who also control your deeds and minds. We, too, have a saying that is more direct and simple to understand—all piles of *drek* stink . . . except our own."

"Just as you say, that is a load of *drek*."

CHAPTER THIRTEEN

The interior of the drying shed was warm and had turned humid. Squared off in the center were Maria and Azim, staring at each other, neither willing to give ground on their beliefs.

Maria said, "We are poor Christians struggling to survive and believe in the rules given to us by our Lord. You have forced me to break many vows this morning by threatening to kill my son. Still, you have no shame, remorse or pity when you ravish me, then hunt children to become slave tributes for a wicked empire. I have sinned this morning, and you have made sure that this burden will rest on my shoulders for the remainder of my days. You are an animal, satisfying your desires with force and threats. To me, that is hardly the way of a *real* man. Rather, it is the way of a brutish savage—the devil's way. And you stand there, justifying all you do, saying you are only following the orders of your ungodly Sultan."

Stunned at the outburst, Azim started at her, anger coursing through him and making him rigid for a moment at her sacrilege and blasphemy. Swiftly, he reached out and struck Maria across the mouth, knocking her to the ground, as her tunics flew up her thighs.

She tasted blood on her lips and responded with a thin smile of scorn, not bothering to rearrange her clothes. "Look at yourself," she jeered. "See the great Turkish aga warrior—head of murdering marauders, priding themselves by overrunning unarmed serfs, then raping defenseless women and imprisoning children. How can such acts make you a proud as a warrior? There is nothing noble in what you do!"

"I have my orders to fulfill for my Sultan," he said, as his expression turned sheepish at the hollow meaning of his words.

"What must your mother think of you, now that you are a Muslim killer, kidnapper and whoremonger? Would she ever welcome you back to your former home knowing what you do? I sincerely believe that the actions of her son would horrify her. Can you imagine standing before her and confessing that you have fallen into the pit of depravity and now pass your life collecting Christian blood as a tax for your Ottoman masters? Have you no decency, no pity for the river of tears and pain that you cause?" Her anger boiled over, as she continued. "You have threatened my son, shamed me, forced me to commit sinful acts and jeopardized my immortal soul. And there you stand before me, naked as a newborn lamb."

"My dear, you are welcome to look and admire, as you wish," he countered, preening unashamedly, then turned around to completely display himself. "As to your immortal soul, go see your priest. He will probably tell you to shout three 'Hail Mary's' and your future mortality will be restored."

Boldly, she stared at his manhood. "Look at that limp ugly thing hanging between your legs. It is shriveled and knotted with veins; all because a dumb peasant woman named Maria stole your first seed. *You Ottoman pig, I will push all of you out of me with my next water.*"

Deeply offended again, he stormed, "Enough, you stinking bitch."

"You did not mind my smell, when you prodded me over and over again," she retorted, brazenly.

"I do Allah's work for my empire. Our lying together was enjoyable for both of us. As I have previously told you, the children we take will be educated and have a far better life than you can ever imagine. You are ignorant and cannot understand that."

"You have made me a fallen woman in the eyes of my God. I can never face my people again. You might as well kill me, for I am not fit to grace my husband's bed, Aga Mathias!"

"*SILENCE!*" the tall man shrieked, "*for you carry both my seed and my child.*"

"*What in the holy name of lunacy are you babbling about? Carry and birth your child! NEVER!*" Maria screamed. "But if that ever did happen, I would go out naked in the snow and stick a knife between my legs, instead of giving birth to *your* bastard."

Her statement stilled his heated talk, and his face became a mask of controlled fury. In a hoarse voice, he replied slowly, "Maria Klobucar, stop the foolishness of thinking only about what is good for you."

"It is my son and family that I think about," she replied heatedly.

Ignoring the interruption, Azim said, "You want to atone for your deeds today. I will tell you what you must do. You will give birth to my child, nourish it and care for it, as though every life in this foul domain of Kostel depends upon it. Do you understand me?"

"More foolish talk from a strutting Turkish idiot," she chided.

"Maria, you are not stupid, so follow my next words closely."

She could tell that his anger was barely in check, evidenced by his piercing stare. That caused her to pause.

"Five years from now, I will return—to harvest the young one that we created today."

Again startled, she responded, "Ha! You force yourself on a woman for the first time, and suddenly you are an oracle who knows the instant a woman is with child. You know nothing about our life and our ways."

"The safety of Kostel lies in your hands," he said with direct simplicity.

Maria missed his point and focused instead on the loss of children in the fiefdom. "Nor do you have any idea how many little ones we lose. Childbirth takes a heavy toll in Kostel, and we lose scores before the priests in our church can confirm them—or even before they can commit any sin. Most men marry when they are in their mid-twenties. Women are a few years younger. Yet, priests, who measure such things, say that the average age of death is twenty-two. That is because we lose so many children. Our cemetery in Fara contains more than I can count—it makes me cry just to remember. In our eyes, it is one of God's miracles, when one of our newborn lives beyond that time and can take his or her place on the family farm."

Azim appeared shocked at this news. Then, he seemed to have a sudden thought, shook his head and wrinkled his nose. Dressing, he commented with unconcealed contempt. "Damn it, woman, you truly are backward, and that goes for your village and this whole region. Has life not taught you and your people anything? Listen to me, for you now carry a part of me with you! Use clean water and strong lye soap to bathe often. It makes no difference how you do it—you can stand in a creek or a wooden bucket, but do it frequently. Our scholars say that simple cleanliness has done wonders, adding years to the lives of our people, and it will do the same for you. You already have one son. Now, you must live for still another."

"Listen to the wise seer from the East," she mocked him, once more. "Besides being a murderer, kidnapper and rapist, you now imagine that you are a healer, as well. Your self-importance is limitless in your eyes."

Azim seemed stung by her derisive cynicism. "For the love of Allah, listen and learn the simple things you can do!"

Maria's expression remained skeptical.

In response, Azim lowered the tone of his voice before continuing. "For example, Maria, I hear that our women dab the ends of a baby's cord with wine after birth so that it heals faster. Also, some say that a drop of wine on a mother's nipples before feeding better assures the child's well-being. In some areas, only tainted water is available, so women boil it before giving it to children. Am Furtt sits downriver from Brod. Who knows what filth runs into the waterway from that town? I have little expertise about such things, but I can tell you that we do not have a high proportion of our children dying early, as you describe it here. Are not these suggestions worth trying? And in fact, there is much to be gained and little to lose."

"Dab my teats with wine before I feed my baby? Only a mad and deranged man would suggest that."

Azim's expression changed. It was now menacing, and he spoke slowly and deliberately. "Understand, Maria, what it means if *you* fail me. Ignore my simple advice, or in any way harm the child you now carry, and I will personally slaughter every living thing in this fiefdom—every animal, every child, every woman and man, and everything that grows. I will level all the farms with fire, including every house and shed throughout Kostel. This land will become a cursed wasteland that everybody will avoid forever, and every traveler will rightly maintain that it is a haunted place with no sunshine—only darkness and ghosts. There will be no warning bonfires when I next return. You will open your door one day, and I will be standing there. Consider my threat carefully, Maria Klobucar! You will not receive another."

Before his angry and terrifying words, she stared at him in stunned silence. The expression on her face changed from defiance to belief. Here was an evil man standing before her who was capable of fully carrying out his threat.

"I, Abdul Azim, Janissary Aga, make this pledge and call upon Allah as my witness. Five years from now, I *will* return! If my son is missing, hurt or abused, I, personally, will crucify you as they did Saint Petar, and then deal with the others in Kostel. Defy me, and even your precious firstborn will not escape my crucifixion wrath. Now, am I making myself exactingly clear?"

"Oh, my God in heaven above," Maria whispered, plainly shaken.

"Have no doubt of what I say. With my men, I am perfectly capable of carrying out my warning." He waited a moment for a reply and, hearing none, he walked to the sleeping boy.

"What are you doing?" she screamed, concern evident in her voice, as she moved quickly to intercept the Turk.

Fending her off with his arm, he bent over and gently picked up the child. Turning, he handed Anton to her.

Wide-eyed with fear, she stared at Azim, her hands trembling, as she took her son and protectively cradled the boy in her arms.

"Damn it, Maria, do we understand each other?" Azim questioned, angrily, his voice rising.

Looking down, she blanched with fear. She nodded. "I believe you are as cruel as you say," she finally said, softly, in reply. "And I know your threat is real."

"Lastly, you will name our new son, Rado, in honor of my most revered Sultan, Murad III. We will speak of this no more!" Turning on his heel, he opened the shed door and walked out into the sunlight.

CHAPTER FOURTEEN

Saint George's Day
Market Kostel
1694

The crowd's mood was uneasy, and this rippled through the gathering. Out of deference to the sensibilities of the bishop, lay priests and the pious in the audience, Johannes omitted the full web of salacious details concerning Maria's seduction in the storage shed during his narration. Even so, his tale captivated serfs, noble gentry and churchmen, without exception. Everyone in Kostel grew up knowing the stories of the raids on Am Furtt and, for many, it struck their hearts with fear.

Gazing at the audience again, Johannes, the Storyteller, said in a softer voice, "It was not easy for the Am Furtt villagers, and indeed, all Kostelians, to return to the lives they had known before that Turkish attack. Those who had lost a child mourned their misfortune. They sought solace from the priests, but mending mortally wounded hearts is a difficult task. Neighbors tried to help, but their efforts largely failed to provide relief. None in the Kostel villages ever stopped grieving over their lost children, yet, as time passed, some of the sharpest pains lessened.

"The burned out sheds meant less grain for the people of Kostel. The loss of fodder represented less food for farm animals during winter months. Serfs died in greater numbers during the snows, particularly the very young and the elderly that year. It took a long time to replace the structures and to return the farming fields to full production. Everyone in the village worked harder and longer for survival.

"Helena recovered from her blow on the head, but from then on, she always referred to Petar as 'my departed husband.' Surprisingly, she insisted on the retrieval of Petar's skull, along with those of all the others, from the tops of wooden stakes lining the Turk's departure route on the other side of the river. It was a gruesome task and reminded villagers of the Turk's ungodliness and inhumanity, preferring acts of cruelty as the means of imposing their will.

"Helena used the family's last silver coins to persuade and hire a passing stranger for the unpleasant task, as Steffan refused his grandmother's request. Once retrieved, the man buried the heads behind her house in a hole that she lined with river rock. To those who inquired, her only response was that someday there would be a returning procession of the dead. Then, she added, 'as you are, we once were; as we are, so shall you be,' repeating a phrase from a well-known ghoulish story about three ghosts encountering three living men walking down a lane. No one was up to challenging her, including her grandson. Figuring that she was temporarily possessed, everyone in the village went about their work and pretended not to notice.

"For Petar's memorial, Helena had the stonecutter at the Fara cemetery carve a simple, modest stone. It was customary in Kostel to keep graveyards small, thereby maximizing the land available to grow crops. It was relatively easy to make space available for the newly deceased by disinterring previous occupants; generally, this happened every five to ten years. As a result, old headstones lined the periphery of the cemetery, like a fence of odd shaped markers. Petar's stone joined this line-up. Every Sunday, Helena made sure flowers or pine boughs decorated his."

Johannes paused, again drinking deeply from his flask. Returning to his instrument, he plucked the strings once more.

"Maria had become pregnant with Anton within months of her marriage to Steffan, as a bond slowly had begun to develop between the newly married couple. They respected each other, but deep affection was not a part of their lives—at least, not yet, and now the Turkish attack suspended the further development of that relationship. It also took time for Steffan to recover from the whipping and regain his previous vigor. He worked the fields and, when others were away, he often broke down and cried, mourning the loss of his *Stari*.

"The young man also tried to make sense of how to deal with the violation of his wife. Neither he nor Maria found it easy to raise the issue, so it festered in both their minds. Steffan felt sorry for her and the abusive treatment she had received at the hands of the Turkish leader. He wanted to comfort her and show greater empathy and be more supportive, but something restrained him—perhaps his pride or self-image. It also affected his pride. The thought of the commander touching her and having his way angered him in a way that he had never felt before.

"On the river, a new barge took form in short order, at the insistence of the Castle Lord of Kostel, as it was a heavily used crossing for trade, and the tolls were an important source of income for Count Petar Erdody. Peasants from every village logged trees from the forest, dragged the trunks to the riverbank and constructed a new ferry in record time.

"During the attack, other women had been abused and severely handled, but Maria found no solace in that knowledge. Only the Turkish commander had raped her; only she and her son were under the threat of being crucified upside-down as was Saint Petar's fate; and only she knew of Azim's threat to lay waste to all of Kostel.

"Helena tried to persuade her to attend the confessional at church to help cleanse her soul, but the young woman rejected the idea. In fact, as the villagers trudged off to Mass every Sunday, Maria remained in the village, often sitting in the meadow, staring at the river. The Turk's ominous words echoed in her head repeatedly, leaving her at a loss at deciding what the better outcome was. Should she hope that she was pregnant—or not? The question went around and around in her head, wondering and worried what the Turkish monster would do to the fiefdom if there were no child—and if one was born, would the little one survive for five years.

"The Catholic Church had worked through its difficulties with sex between men and women over many centuries after Adam and Eve committed the original sin by consuming from the *tree of knowledge of good and evil*. After all, reproduction is natural and is the way God intends all of us to beget future generations. Catholic religious doctrine considers marriage to be a rite of passage and sacrament—holding that a couple's relationship uniquely expresses an unbreakable bond equal to the love between Christ and His people.

"Steffan and Maria's wedding ceremony, with the priest's blessing, assured the newly married couple that they had the Church's consent to mate, without fear that it was sinful, even if the act of procreation was lustful. The church maintains that sex after matrimony is compulsory, as it joins man and woman into one flesh. Therefore, each owes it to the other to comply, when one wants intimacy, and refusing such a request dishonors the obligation that marriage places on each. Lastly, marriage symbolizes the unbreakable bond of Christ to the Church, and similarly, a wedded couple has the same unbreakable bond to each other.

"In spite of these religious bonds of matrimony, Maria continually refused Steffan at night when he sought her.

"She missed two womanly cycles and, in one sense, began to feel relieved that the question regarding pregnancy was answered. At other times, she was sickened at the thought of giving birth to the monster's baby. Her quickening came in the fourth month, feeling the baby move inside her, and knowing for sure that she was with child. With that knowledge, she became even more depressed. The Turk's prophecy was a living and growing curse within her body. If there were no complications, the birth would occur before the Easter celebration in the new year. It also made her think about the man's warning of returning in five years and destroying everything in the fiefdom if anything happened to his sired child. These memories invariably found its way into her daily thoughts."

Johannes' voice turned softer as he gazed at the gathering. "Nearly half of the winter's food supply for farm animals was lost in the torched drying sheds. This resulted in the people slaughtering their animals early, then salting or drying the meat, to preserve as much as possible. Usually, villagers avoid cutting grasses near the riverbank, as it was farther to carry the heavy loads, adding more work to their busy days. An added concern was the danger of striking rocks along the edge of the river, which can severely damage, or even destroy, the curved metal blades of a scythe—a tool upon which all farmers depend on, particularly at harvesting time. Still, my friends, Am Furtt villagers did what was necessary, as men mowed wild grass and millet that grew along the river. Villagers stuffed remaining sheds and barns to the brim, and then they added more, hoping to shelter as much fodder as possible from the coming rains and winter snows.

"With two dozen hides in the village, that amounted to over two hundred acres of wheat in Am Furtt that needed to be cut yearly by hand. The cut stalks dried lying in the fields, then were transported to the sheds and barns. Lastly, grain and stalks are sorted. Am Furtt, like the other farming hamlets in Kostel, used the open field system, as you serfs know, to manage common lands planted in grain or pasture. Thus, the entire wheat harvest is a chore shared by all adult villagers and older children in the region, not just a single village. To repay those from other hamlets, serfs reciprocated the labor. Harvesting grain is hot, strenuous work, with the beating sun, buzzing insects and hay dust clinging to sweaty bodies, causing everyone to itch.

"Cutting began at first light, and Maria carried a basket containing a single glass, a jug of *rakia*, smoked sausages and bread to feed the men in the field. Helena stayed at the house cooking the breakfast of sliced ham, greens, fried onions and beer. In the meadows, men sharpened their blades by drawing whetstones along the cutting edges of the scythes. Blades need to be sharp, as you know, to reduce the effort to pull it through its mowing arc. Men frequently stopped during the day to use the sharpening stones.

"After eating, men loosened their muscles with several practice swings. Then, grasping the twin handholds mounted on the wooden shaft, they began cutting, keeping the blade six to eight inches above the ground. Women and older children followed and raked the cut wheat into lines along the ground. Every day, women and children turned over the lines to aid the drying process. As every villager here knows, time is crucial at this point of the harvest, as any sudden rainstorm causes mildew to develop, which can destroy the crop.

"For the journey back to barns and sheds, wheat sheaves were bundled and tied with stems, the same as is done today, and then loaded onto large linen tarps. Women and older children carried the sixty-to-seventy-pound packs in one of two ways—strapped across their shoulders on their backs, or on top of their heads, with a small straw pad to cushion the big bundle. Both methods look ungainly, but most women preferred the second method by carrying the loads on their head. The sheds, with their well-ventilated sidewalls, completed the drying process.

"Before filling the sheds, the villagers separated the precious harvest of grain from the chaff by beating the stalks against a lean-to screen, which allowed seeds to fall through while blocking the larger matter such as the stalks. Those who had a storage shed or a barn with a wooden floor used a horse or ox to crush and separate the material by having the animal walk in continuous circles on the stalks. A boy often saw that the animal continued moving by flicking a switch as encouragement. For greater refinement, breezy days were selected to heave the cuttings into the air from tarps, thereby letting the husks and lighter chaff blow away while the heavier grain fell back to the cloth.

"Grain is a major food and becomes bread and pasta, as well as feed for chickens and livestock. Everyone knew that the next few years would bring food shortages and difficult times. Further, three to four acres of hay are required to feed and maintain one cow during the winter months. Some of these animals might not survive the coming winter despite being a prized possession.

"Cows and goats provided milk to make cheese. This task in the Klobucar household fell to Maria, and that year, she added a greater supply of cheese to the larder to supplement food supplies. After each milking, she put aside a portion in a separate pot and covered it with a cloth, allowing the milk to sour. Afterward, she heated it and strained out the curds. She kneaded the mixture, added salt and herbs, rolled it into a ball or cheese wheel and let it set.

"The young woman did her usual chores and tended to the lash cuts on Steffan's back. Yet, her usually bright, friendly spirit had disappeared, and she infrequently spoke unless replying to a question. As the days passed, she despaired about the future of Kostel and the fear of losing Anton, family and neighbors, as well as her immortal soul. Additionally, her pregnancy nearly drove her to distraction. On one side, her motherly instincts reveled in the thought of a new baby. Then, a cloud seemed to descend, as the image of Mathias, the monster Turkish commander, filled her mind. She remembered him standing before her, his naked arrogance on display."

Johannes paused, and then added, "Observing her, Helena became increasingly concerned. One day, when they were alone, the older woman said, 'Maria, I am here for you. You know you can talk with me.' Maria made no reply, yet she understood that it was only a matter of time before everyone in the village would know that she was with child. Even so, the time was not right for her. Helena did not push the matter, and the days passed. Helena advised her that the Church could help, and that contrition and confession were good for the soul and for her peace of mind. The younger woman nodded in agreement. Even so, her self-torment intensified with the secret shame locked deep within her."

CHAPTER FIFTEEN

Am Furtt
<u>1580</u>

One sunny afternoon in October, Helena said, "Let us walk," and placed her arm firmly around Maria's shoulders, guiding the young woman across the fields to a drying shed. "It is time for you to unburden yourself and talk to me—and to God," she advised.

"You are probably right," Maria responded, "but I feel such shame and deep humiliation. I feel it in the very core of my body."

"Take your time, my child. Just know that speaking the words helps. You already know that I am here for you."

"I appreciate all that you are doing, Nana Helena. I really do. Still, it is so hard for me to unburden myself."

The older woman watched her carefully. Then, she said, "It was in one of the sheds where the Turk took you. Am I right, my child?"

Tears ran down Maria's face and answered the question as the young woman buried her face in the older woman's shoulder. "Oh, Nana, it was . . . yes, it was in a shed that Anton and I were taken—one that was burned down."

"There, there," Helena crooned. "Your concerns will come out when they are ready. But, please try to do it before the new child arrives."

Startled and drawing back, Maria gaped at the older woman, as tears continued to fill her eyes. "You know? How is that possible? I have told no one, not even Steffan?"

"I did not know, but I suspected. Just calm yourself and tell me what happened."

Maria sobbed softly. After a while, the words began, haltingly at first. She told Helena how the Turkish aga had chased her and Anton on horseback and flung them to the ground before hurrying them into the shed. Then, the young woman relayed the Turk's rambling details about how many white Christian children were converted to Islam before they became Janissary warriors or held other posts for the Sultan in the Turkish Empire.

Helena was round-eyed with amazement as she tried to picture Maria's description of the vast number of white slaves in the Ottoman Empire. "They have as many as we have stalks of wheat in our fields?" she repeated. "Oh my God, how horrible these people are!"

The young woman nodded, then went on to recite the composition of the Turk's troop, again expressing confusion about the reason why the man had spoken of such matters to her. "And, Nana Helena," she continued, "I sinned when I lay with a man who is not my husband. God will punish me, and rightly so. I shame myself just thinking about it. The Turk threatened Anton. He said that if I did not obey him, he would bash your great-grandson's head against a wooden pillar in the shed. I was so scared for my little boy." Crimson with shame and self-loathing, the young woman hung her head and continued in a weak voice, as she stared at the ground. "I can never be the same woman to Steffan. The barbarian debased me, and I violated the laws of our religion. And, on top of all else, I have sacrificed my immortal soul."

"Yes, you must make peace with God. The way to begin is in the church confessional. Our Lord is merciful. He will forgive you because you had to go to great lengths to save your child. I firmly believe that there are ways to save your mortal soul, but you must first go to Fara and talk with the bishop."

Maria stared at her and then nodded. "I would like to believe that, but I have been so torn and . . ."

"I know, dear Maria," Helena interrupted. She feared that the young woman would lose her nerve and stop talking to her. "Trust me, I will always tell you the truth. I will go with you to Fara in the morning. Is there anything else about the Turkish attack that you have not said to me?"

"That man—the Turkish commander—his name is Aga Abdul Azim. Mathias is his former Christian name. He said that if any harm befalls the baby, he will kill everyone in Kostel, beginning by crucifying Anton and me, just as Saint Petar was tortured and murdered. He also said that he and his men would burn down every village and structure in the fiefdom and destroy every living thing so that Kostel becomes a wasteland, and all future travelers will forever think that the land is cursed and haunted by the ghosts of villagers who once lived here."

"Josip e Maria—Joseph and Mary!" Helena exclaimed. The unimaginable horror stunned the old woman, and a long silence fell between them, each lost in her own

thoughts. Finally, Helena said, "You must tell Steffan everything. He may already suspect about the baby. Do not keep anything from him. I assure you that he will understand, given the terrible ordeal that all of us have experienced."

"Oh, Nana, this is so hard for me to do."

"Hush—hush, dear. You realize that the Turkish soldier was a bastard who forced you against your will, for that is the only way he can have satisfaction with a woman. He does not live by the rule of God. Take courage, my child."

Turning away, Maria walked a few steps and sat down on a keg. "I wish to heaven that was all there was to it," she blurted out.

Helena waited silently, realizing that Maria needed to unburden herself in a manner and time that suited her. Only then would she begin to bind her soul together and come to a place of peace with herself. So, she just said, "Take your time, my dear. You had no choice—you wanted to save your son. The Turk forced you, and yours was a selfless act of courage to save your child. You were very brave."

"No, you do not understand what I mean. The Turk told me things that I never . . . I never even imagined."

Both remained silent, as Helena found a barrel and sat across from the young woman.

"He told me that Janissary rules forbid them to lay with a woman—rules that had been in place for more than one hundred years and were strictly enforced. He told me that every male needs a release for his passion and, I should know this having lived on a farm all my life. Instead of women, the Janissaries use boys or other men. Nana, I have never heard or imagined such things."

The revelation took Helena by surprise, although she had heard whispers from time to time about certain priests. She remained silent.

"He said that the self-denial rule had recently changed. Then . . . he demanded that . . . I show him the proper way to lay with a woman ... and I was to do it willingly and fully, or he would end Anton's life instantly, right there in the shed. Oh, Nana, it is so hard for me to repeat his words."

Helena was sure that a look of shock was evident on her face, and she turned aside quickly to regain her composure and not show her astonishment. In a weak voice, she said, "Go on. Again, you must never forget that the man forced himself on you, and you were protecting your son. No one can misjudge you for such a sacrifice."

Maria nodded once more, yet her expression was one of dejection. Slowly, she resumed. "So, I willed myself to do as he asked—the first time we lay together. Then, there was a second. But, the third time ... Holy Mother of God ... my body reacted on its own, and I found myself responding to the evil Turk, even when my mind said to stop the sinful madness. I could not control my feelings ... and did not want to ... at that instant. Now, dear Nana, you can understand why my immortal soul is in such great peril. I shame myself in telling you these things, but now you know that I have thrown away any opportunity for salvation."

"Good God, Almighty!" Helena exclaimed.

"I am truly a fallen woman and unfit for the bed of your grandson. On top of that, I bear another man's child, and this baby's well-being may affect every living thing in the fief. Oh Nana Helena, now you know why my spirits have been so low."

Helena stood and hurried to Maria as she recovered her composure. She hugged the young woman, stroking her hair gently. "Dear, you have been through so much that you do not fully understand. You must listen to me! None of us can undo the day of the attack. I will never have my dear departed husband back, and you now know things that you never imagined. You and I must live for our children. They are our wealth, and they are the reason God placed us on this land—to raise, care for and love them. That is the job you and I have, for Anton and the new one."

Maria drew back and tearfully looked at her. "But Nana Helena, I wish no part of any child that grows in me from the seed that the Turkish bastard planted!"

Helena was astonished and shocked once more. She drew the woman into her arms again. Softly, she said, "You will see it differently as the time for birthing draws closer. Remember, the little one will also be your flesh and blood—and it will be your milk and your love that will nourish the baby. As to your soul, such acts have certainly occurred before. After all, the Turks have been raiding Kostel for the past one hundred years—maybe even longer. You will go to see the bishop, and I will go with you. Through contrition, confession and penance, he will guide us. I am sure of it. And, I will be right beside you to help."

Helena noticed that her soothing words appeared to comfort the younger woman.

Then, as though recalling Azim's last words, Maria exclaimed, "But the bastard swore that he would return in five years for his child. He was the very essence of naivety, still his over-sized ego convinced him that the spilling of his first seed conceived a child—he never wavered in this belief. As a result, he *will* return one day. I just know it! Oh, Nana, what are we to do?"

A feeling of furious rage was building within Helena, as she continued to comfort the girl. The many details of Maria's experience staggered her. Despite this, she knew that she had to be strong and that the young woman needed her more than ever. She made a resolution as she continued to stroke Maria's back. *Never, again, will we submit like sheep to the slaughter by those evil men. I am not sure what we can do, but we will find a way.*

To the girl, she answered, "Have faith! There will be a way. Still, there is one thing you need to know and to believe. No man is going to take the new baby away from you—not Aga Azim, nor anyone else! Do you hear me? *NO ONE!* I believe that with everything inside me, and you must as well. You and I will find a way. You have my solemn pledge before God on that!"

Maria managed a faint smile through her glistening tears.

"Now, you can start to heal. You have lanced the boil inside you, and it begins draining the ugly puss from your soul. Tomorrow, we will go to Fara and the church. You must make peace with God and know what penance the bishop will impose. As for my grandson, you are the most courageous woman that he will ever know. Never hang your head before him. Steffan will not beat you nor turn you out of our house. If anything, he should kneel down and bless his wife for saving Anton. As for the gossips," Helena reminded the younger woman, "when you bite your tongue, remember someone is talking about you. Let them! Just bite your sleeve, and they, in turn, will bite their own tongues. It is your life that matters, along with the new baby."

Trembling and trying to smile through tearful eyes, Maria looked at Helena with gratitude. "I love you Nana, and thank you for being so understanding."

"There is one more thing, Maria. The Turk is mad, but his threat cannot remain a secret from our neighbors in the village or others in Kostel. They must know of the possible danger."

Maria looked at the ground and then nodded. "Yes, his words were direct, and the matter affects all who live in the fief. Nana, will you help me do it?"

"Yes, of course, my dear. You have had enough on your shoulders. I will repeat Aga Azim's words to them. I suppose we must do the same with the Castle Lord. We will need his cooperation."

"Again, thank you for your kindness and help."

The two remained in the shed for some time. In the course of their discussion, Helena learned more about Aga Azim's force of six Janissaries, with the rest of his troop comprised of either slaves or irregular Bosnian bandits. She found the information enlightening. It would be useful in the plan that was beginning to take form in her mind.

As they were about to leave, Helena asked a question, which had been nagging at her. "Maria, I know you went alone to Černá Creek when you delivered Anton. Do you wish my help when the new baby arrives?"

Helena knew many women worked throughout the day before delivering their baby. And, much like ancient Greek mythology concerning the Illyrian people, it was traditional for the mother to be alone at birthing time—somewhere out of the house, sparing everyone the mother's distress and inevitable clean-up. Further, the Illyrian myth held that the woman would wrap the newborn in swaddling clothes, then bring the child to the village and say that she had found it on the side of the road. All would marvel at the miracle and comment with admiration.

"Thank you, I would like your help," Maria said.

"Have you selected a place yet? The creek will be frozen, and the fields will be equally cold at that time of year."

For the first time, Maria's eyes were bright. "Nana, I will give birth in a drying shed—this one. It is a fitting place."

"All right. Will you let me make the needed preparations so that everything will be ready when your time comes?"

"Thank you. Yes, I welcome that."

"And I have changed my mind about some of the advice I gave you earlier. Tell Steffan everything—except the last time the Turk forced you. Husbands should know most things but not everything." Smiling, Helena hugged

Maria and whispered into her ear, "Raise your head, my daughter. You and I are going to war against the invaders, and we begin right now."

Shutting the door behind them, the women walked arm-in-arm to the farmhouse.

CHAPTER SIXTEEN

Helena informed her neighbors about the Turk's threat following the completion of the harvest. They were horrified at the prospect and resented the fact that the Turk promised to return, specifically, to collect Maria's child, thereby jeopardizing all. The news spread throughout the fiefdom and was soon on everyone's lips. Village elders in various hamlets discussed the issue and expressed frustration, yet none seemed to have solutions.

Helena knew such talk was circulating in Kostel. She also knew that it would take strong leadership to coalesce the many viewpoints into plans for action. She discussed these with Maria but held back some of her deepest views, concerned that it would overly unnerve the pregnant woman.

Life continued. Other chores demanded attention, even with the harvest completed. Helena loved this time of year, when dried yellow bedstraw flowers replaced former stuffing in mattresses. The new filling had the sweet-smelling scent of mowed hay and, further, acted as a flea killer. Dried petals also yielded yellow dye and helped coagulate milk in making cheese. With the ripening and malt production of hops, Steffen began brewing *pivo*—beer, which was a staple drink for all meals and all occasions. Other than wine and *rakia*, adults preferred it to water or milk. Besides hops—dandelions, burdock root, marigold and other herbs—provided flavorings for the beer. Some villagers preferred using gruit, which was a combination of sweet gale, mugwort, yarrow or ground ivy. Her grandson leaned toward horehound, heather, cinnamon or even aniseed.

Helena, dressed in her mourning black, watched Maria, as the young woman went about her daily work. She sensed that Maria was trying not to believe the Turk's threat, perhaps laying it at the feet of an arrogant man who had tasted the lips of a woman for the first time.

Maria performed her chores without thinking, while carrying a tremendous burden of guilt, despite unburdening herself to Steffan and the bishop. Helena traveled with her on two occasions to the small St. Bartholomew's Catholic Church in the City of Gottschee. The sermons were in German, as the area had carried over traditions from its Bavarian roots. It was an ordeal for both women to make the sixty mile round trip by horse and cart, but they realized that their bishop had prescribed a difficult penance for the very purpose of allowing Maria to redeem her immortal soul. Thus, it had a spiritual importance beyond measure for Maria.

Helena and Maria made the journeys, but it cut into the time they devoted to farm chores, as each trip took several days. Nonetheless, they completed the visits in three months, by which time Maria was heavy with child. Helena helped the young woman fight through periods of depression and was always present to console her.

The month of December arrived, and it was a time for celebrating *kolinje*, the annual slaughtering of the village's pigs before Christmas. Helena always looked forward to this celebration. Even though she saw most of her neighboring villagers daily, *kolinje* was an annual tradition of renewing relationships with friends.

On that day, Helena and Maria were in the kitchen early, preparing breakfast for Steffan, his brothers and Ivan, who was the butcher. All of the men were dressed warmly against the cold, wearing gray or brown woolen cloaks, thick woolen leggings wrapped around their feet and legs and leather clogs; additionally, linen aprons covered them in front from head to foot. A chill was in the air, and frost covered the ground under skies that were gray and threatening. The men, standing next to the family's pigpen, slapped their arms against their sides to keep warm, and their chilled breath formed clouds around the words they exchanged in the early morning air.

Maria, also walking on clogs over the frozen ground outside, carried a jug of heated *rakia* to warm the men and a drinking mug. First, she served the butcher, who was the honored guest. She filled the goblet to the brim.

"*Živio!*" Ivan toasted long life to his companions, finishing the warm fiery drink in one gulp. Next, Maria wiped out the tumbler with her apron and served the others in the order of their age. Each man swallowed the strong, fiery liquor, and gave his own salutation for long life to his friends.

Sturdy tree limbs, closely driven into the ground, made up the sides of the pigpen fence. Rawhide strips tightly bound them together. Steffan threw a loop over the largest pig, and the men dragged it out of the pen. The trio fell on it, struggling to hold it down while the butcher slashed the animal's throat. An instant later, Helena slid a shallow wooden trough beneath the cut to collect the blood.

After the final death throes, Steffan covered the animal with dry straw and leaves gathered from the forest and then set it ablaze to burn off the pig's tough bristles from the hide. Next, with thick ropes tied around each of the animal's hind legs, the men wrestled the big animal high up onto a tripod.

Helena watched from the house as the butcher set out his tools, which included knives, ax, hammer and saw. With the animal's liver in hand, she saw Maria return to the house to begin preparing the traditional soup for lunch.

Both women repeatedly carried out buckets of boiling water, as the men cleaned the carcass and scraped the skin. As the animal slowly became cuts of meat, the men hefted these on their shoulders and carried them into the house and up the interior stairs to the attic. There, it was stored, and the curing process began, using smoke from the fireplace below, which rose through a hole in the ceiling and drifted into the attic before escaping through the thrush roofing. Thus, the area was always warm and dry.

Kolinje produced the family's primary source of meat for the following year, including black pudding and fried cracklings. In addition to pork, other meats occasionally supplemented their meals, such as chicken, roasted mutton, wild game and fish.

A large black iron kettle hung from a tripod over a roaring wood fire at the back of the yard, as far away as possible from the house and the men butchering the animal. The pot began the rendering process of turning layers of animal fat into lard, which the family used for many purposes. These included cooking, a spread for bread, candle making and general lubricant, such as cart axles. It also produced especially unpleasant smells; hence, the distant location of the iron vessel.

The men paused, each lifting another glass of *rakia*, which Maria carried outside, and, again, she began by serving Ivan first.

"Hey, you Klobucars, this is a fine looking animal," the butcher commented, "with an excellent layer of fat." Soon news about the size, condition and thickness of the animal spread throughout Am Furtt. Neighbors came to watch the butcher at work. The village family with the pig having the heaviest layer of fat had the bragging rights for having raised the best animal during the rest of the long winter.

"We have much to cook today," Helena commented to Maria. "First, the soup, then we will roast ribs and cook the brain for our feast tonight in celebration of our excellent pig," she said, smiling. "Afterward, we will make our links of blood sausages" Creating the links involved mixing the animal's blood, freshly ground pork and seasoning, stuffed into clean pig intestines as casings.

Maria said, "I am leaving now, Nana, to go down to the river with some of the village children to clean the intestines. I promised to roast some for the little ones tomorrow, as a treat." Both knew the blood had to be used the same day to prevent it from spoiling.

"All right, but remind them that cleaning the insides must be done carefully and thoroughly."

"Of course, Nana."

After supervising the washing, Maria returned to the house, hauling a tub of the gray and white entrails.

"How goes the cleaning," Helena asked, brushing aside a strand of hair that had fallen across her brow.

"It is all done. A few of the younger ones wanted to quit because the river water is so cold at this time of year. I reminded them about Milo, whose job last year was to stomp cabbage in the sauerkraut barrel. Remember, Nana, the boy's lips turned blue from the cold kraut."

Both women laughed at the memory.

The gathering in their home was festive that evening. Helena noticed her grandson's wife laughing and mixing well with the group, which was a first since Petar's death and the attack. They feasted on the meat, boiled turnips, noodles, and later, various cakes washed down with white wine fermented two months earlier.

Later, Helena and Maria stuffed blood sausages, with the help of the butcher's wife. They broke out in laughter each time a skin ripped, squirting out the dough mixture of congealed blood, meat, lard and spices. Late that night, after stuffing the last one, Maria roasted some on the grill to give everyone a taste. It marked the end of a very long day for everyone.

Helena knew that considerable work remained during the following week. They had to finish rendering the lard and making the differently seasoned fillings for other pork sausages. In the attic, many different cuts of meat hung from the rafters, including row after row of mottled looking, red-colored sausages, strung to each other and draped from poles attached to roof beams. The hanging kielbasas looked like decorations for a party and created a festive look in the attic.

The women prepared each rear leg joint to cure as ham, by making a brine mixture—including herbs and crystallized honey. The ingredients went into a wooden barrel for each hindquarter, then the barrel was sealed and left to cure for several weeks in the very cold temperature of the barn. Then, the joints were slowly baked in a stone oven.

Throughout the busy days, Helena watched Maria, as the girl dutifully went about her daily chores. Often, the younger woman stopped to place a hand on her distended abdomen, as though it soothed the inner child. Helena renewed her vow that no one was going to steal Maria's newborn, and her newest great-grandchild. It was not going to happen! The question she kept pondering was how to prevent it.

As she milked the cow one morning, Helena's thoughts turned over the problem of how to defend the village against the next Turkish raid. *These are indeed difficult times,* she thought, *still our Kostelian kin and friends have called on our inner strength and our faith in God to see us through the worst. Even so, I see the despair left in the aftermath of the last attack. It is the time that I take matters into my own hands...!*

CHAPTER SEVENTEEN

On Christmas day, Helena stunned her family. She arose that morning and discarded her black mourning clothes, entering the great room wearing a white tunic with a blood-red bodice.

Wide-eyed with surprise, Steffan exclaimed, "Nana Helena, you are breaking tradition the way you are dressed. Everyone will know that you are disrespecting grandfather's memory! How can you do such a thing? All the villagers will wonder if you have become a 'grass widow,' secretly looking for another husband."

"Bah! Let them think what they will. As for me searching for a new husband, all know that I am beyond such foolishness at my age. Besides, no one could replace my dear departed husband. The important thing now is that all of us must move on with our lives. We have another Turkish attack confronting us in a few years. We must use the time to make plans and take actions. Maria, you, too, must wear something more colorful. I release you from wearing black. From this day forward, this family will let the past take care of itself, live with the good memories that we have and look to the future."

Helena's choice of clothes astounded other villagers, and indeed, all Kostelians were shocked. Black was the symbol of mourning, ingrained as a tradition over the centuries. For some, breaking it was unsettling—only loose and shameless women refused to mourn for the dead and threw off their black habits. Still, that view was hard to reconcile with the Helena everyone knew. After a few weeks, the villagers' minds began to change, and they looked upon her action as a new breath of life in the small hamlet that had lost two children and drying sheds, and where many men carried scars on their backs from the lashes.

Saturday was market day. Helena, dressed in her bright clothes, and the family set off for Market Kostel. They packed the horse with an extra pork leg joint and other goods to trade with vendors, particularly for salt. It was the one mineral needed to sustain all animal life, including people, and there were no known deposits in Kostel or anywhere in the region. Therefore, imported shipments came from evaporation ponds located along the Adriatic coast. Because of its rarity and absolute necessity, people often referred to it as "white gold."

The Klobucars arrived before mid-morning and set up shop in the shadow of the castle. Helena let Steffan and Maria do the bartering, as she kept watch on the iron gate, which was deep-set in the castle wall, and through which Count Petar Erdody was likely to appear. She had matters to discuss with the man, and she waited impatiently for him to appear. It was the first time since the Turkish attack that such an opportunity had presented itself to her.

Helena was aware that it was the Count's routine to walk through the marketplace during the morning hours, acknowledging some with a regal flair and gauging the production of his serfs. He was not a large man, and he wore his graying hair tied off at his shoulders. His wrinkled, bearded face and dark eyes evidenced little warmth. On cold days, such as that one, he donned a fur-lined coat, gaily-patterned wool leggings and a bearskin hat with flaps that covered his ears.

Finally, she saw him walk through the gate. As usual, his steward was at his side, followed by the new captain of the guard and several ladies from the Lord's court. Count Erdody was a hard master, demanding that his serfs pay an increasing amount of taxes. It was evident by his dress that he was suffering little, while his people had difficulty surviving, following the Turkish attack.

Helena placed herself directly in the Count's path. As he came close, she bowed but looked up quickly. "My Lord, Count Erdody," she began, "you know that the commander of the last Turkish raid has vowed to return in five years. Do you have a plan that will better defend Kostel at that time?"

The surprised reaction on the man's face was not difficult to read. His immediate irritation showed as the color rose on his face, and his mouth curled down in anger at the interruption of his stroll.

"Eh, who are you, woman, to ask me such an audacious question, here in the middle of *my* public marketplace and at this time?"

"I am Helena Klobucar, from Am Furtt," she said, her words emitting mists of vapor on that cold morning. "I lost my dear departed husband to the Turkish bastards during the raid, and our village lost two children. We also lost drying sheds, which the Turks burned, including the hay and fodder stored inside. Additionally, some of our men were whipped. You knew my dearly departed husband, as our family operates the ferry at the Am Furtt crossing and collects your tolls." The air was bitterly cold, and everyone's breath was visible, as she stared directly at the Lord of the

Castle. "Beg pardon, Count Erdody, but I ask once more, what are your plans to defend this fiefdom when the Turks return? How will you be better prepared?"

The castle steward stepped forward to move Helena out of his master's way. Immediately, Steffen and other men closed ranks behind her, even though all were shocked at Helena confronting the Lord of Kostel.

"I am sorry for the losses, but it could not be helped," the elderly Lord answered. "Surely, you are aware that the market village and castle also came under attack. I lost good men, too, including Captain of the Guard."

"I truly am sorry for that, and I will pray for their souls at Mass on Sunday," Helena said. "Did you send any soldiers to pursue the Turks and try to recover our abducted children?"

"Madam, I could not give such an order, as I had no way of knowing if they would return and attack once more."

"Then, you sent out scouts to track the raiders. Is that right?"

Count Erdody stared at her angrily, as his flushed expression deepened, despite the cold winter temperature, his rapid breathing clearly visible.

"From your expression, I take it that you sent no one!" Helena noted, disdain apparent in her voice. "So, what is the plan when the Turks return? Your serfs have a right to know."

"I do not discuss war plans with serfs and certainly not with an old woman in my domain," the Count replied, sarcastically.

"All right, here is my grandson, Steffan," she said, taking the young man's arm and pulling him forward. "Explain it to him. And I, a humble serf woman of limited knowledge, will try to follow and understand the complexity of your words and your thoughts on how this fiefdom can be better defended when the Turks next attack Kostel."

The Count stared at her for a moment. Drawing himself up, he said with a sneer, "Your interruption of my walk this morning is intolerable. As for the possibility of future attacks, we have only the word of one serf, and a *woman* at that, from your village. Therefore, we have no credible information from spies and soldiers."

"Exactly how many advance notices do you require, My Lord? Surely, one is better than none."

"Peasant woman, you severely try my patience. Get thee gone!"

"Or perhaps, there is no plan," Helena persisted, her anger rising. Lifting her arm and shaking her fist in the general direction of the castle, she asked, "Is that your answer? Your serfs are simply to wait, like docile lambs, when again, farms are burned, women are ravaged, village men feel the lash of the whip and our precious children are plucked from our farms like chickens from their roosts. And all the while, you sit on your arse in the castle, protected by walls that are six feet thick, and guarded by the castle's towers, cannons and soldiers." Raising her voice even louder, she continued, "Everyone here today has a right to know the answer to my question! You owe this to the people of Kostel!"

"Madam, your tongue cuts deeply, and it wags faster than a mongrel dog's tail. Tread carefully, or you, too, may feel the waspish bite of the whip."

By then, all trading had stopped in the marketplace, evidencing the concern and interest of Kostelians, who crowded around. Traders from other parts of the empire also listened with great interest, as the exchange provided juicy morsels of gossip for their upcoming journeys to other bazaars.

Bishop Juris was among the many who watched, as the discussion played out. He stepped forward, raised the golden crucifix hanging from his neck and made the sign of the cross with his free hand. "Helena Klobucar, your comments are insulting to our Fiefdom Lord, Count Erdody. You know very well about the attacks on the castle and Marketplace Kostel. There was severe damage, including the church losing its bell tower in the fire. Three bells crashed to the ground and cracked. I think under the circumstances, you might be more forgiving and understanding in your comments."

"Honorable Bishop Juris, I asked the castle lord a simple question—does he have a plan for defending this fiefdom better when the Turks next attack us? Do you not think this is worthy of an answer? And, that is especially concerning for the people who lost so much in the last assault?"

"Of course, my child," the bishop commented, noting the growing number of people gathered around them. "I am sure such information will be forthcoming. Am I right, Count Erdody?"

"In due time, perhaps, but my main charge from Vienna is to maintain and protect the Gottschee-to-Delnice road, which ties together port towns on the Adriatic Sea to the capital city of Vienna and the rest of the Empire. I must keep that uppermost in my thoughts, and plan accordingly."

"And, how does one best do that?" Helena asked, in a tone now void of respect that bordered on mockery. "Does it just occur out of the air, My Lord? Perhaps, such deep and complicated thoughts arise when you and your men play bocce ball inside the stone walls of the castle!"

The gathered people let out a loud guffaw at the witty turn of phrase.

"Damn you, woman," the Count said, fed up with the insults. "I have already informed you that Vienna expects me to protect that vital roadway."

"Everyone knows that fact, including the Turks," she said, her voice again rising. The man's avoidance of the question clearly irked her. "Furthermore," she continued, "everyone knows that the Kupa River at Am Furtt is the strategic point where raiders cross to attack our lands. Defend it, and you defend all of Kostel, as well as the villages and towns farther north. How is it that this fact is so difficult to comprehend? So, I ask again about a plan, My Lord?"

"This woman impudence knows no bounds," the Count answered loudly, his patience exhausted. "Your next word will bring the cat-o'-nine-tails across your back, old woman! Do you hear me? Silence that churlish tongue of yours!"

Undeterred, Helena stood her ground. "Your soldiers must have seen the signal fire on the hill from the high walls of the castle, as did everyone in Kostel. Even so, you sent no soldiers to protect the serfs working your lands, neither that evening nor the next morning. We had to fend for ourselves while you sheltered behind high walls. All of Kostel knows the Turks will return—and you know it, too. How can it be that you refuse to answer my question—a question that is on the minds of all in this fiefdom!"

"Guards, seize this mad woman! Her tortuous drivel spews forth like a never-ending river of sewage."

Helena raised her arms in frustration. "We have a right to know!" Turning to the people surrounding them, she appealed, "Do you think I am right?"

There was a rousing, loud response, and many people applauded.

"Child," began Bishop Juris. "I think..."

"Think what, Father? What care I if your precious bells fall to the ground compared to losing our children! Forges recast church bells all the time—nothing brings back our lost children! Tell all of us, where were you during the attack? Were you standing in front of your church, waving the cross draped around your neck and protecting your precious church bells?"

Red in the face with embarrassment, the priest went mute.

"Well, were you standing there?" Helena persisted loudly.

"I was in the castle," the bishop said meekly.

"We have a large group here today. I do not think the crowd in the marketplace heard you. Can you speak up, Holy Father?"

Louder, the holy man said, "I was at the Count's side, in the castle."

"Well, that makes two bold, courageous men defending the Fiefdom of Kostel from the marauders by hiding inside castle walls."

A loud rumble arose from the crowd, as some laughed while others muttered angrily.

"Child, you must . . ."

"Oh, for heaven's sake, Father, stop calling me child. I am easily old enough to be your mother or even your grandmother!" Opening her arms wide to dramatize her point, Helena stepped forward. "The first target of any future Turkish attack will be the river crossing at Am Furtt. Until the Castle Lord, our priests and everyone recognize and accept that fact, there can be no effective plan. I have said my piece. Count, we serfs will expect to hear your plan within the next few months—let us say, by the time we celebrate Easter."

The older man flushed anew with anger. He took a step back, as he observed the size of the crowd and the number of traders from distant places. He also appeared to remember his status as Lord of the Fiefdom and apparently figured it best to avoid publically cursing this impertinent woman before all of his other serfs. With obvious difficulty, he controlled himself. As it already stood, the traveling traders would soon spread the entertaining and gossipy news of this encounter when an aged woman challenged the Lord of the Castle in *his* own marketplace—and held her ground. The encounter might even make it to the ears of those who served on the Supreme Council in Vienna.

Seeing his expression, Helena continued, driving her point home. "And we expect you to get the money from Vienna, or use your personal fortune, to pay for the added defenses, for that is the nobility's duty." With that, she turned and began walking away.

"I have had enough of this public interrogation," the Count stormed, and he, too, turned back toward the castle gate.

Hearing the last comment, Helena angrily spun around to face the man once more, and shouted in a harsh voice, "Who among you can write? I wish to send a letter to Vienna, informing the Emperor that we remain unprotected from attacks in Kostel and that there is no plan to deal with the next one. Furthermore, that the Lord of the Castle is uncaring about his people, and he even refuses to discuss the matter or share his thoughts. Who, among you, will compose the letter for me?"

Again, Count Erdody turned and stared at the old woman. His eyes were narrow slits, close set in his bewhiskered face, and the expression on his face was dark with fury. "You have stirred quite enough trouble for one day, Helena Klobucar. Take thee back to your village and keep your opinions to yourself. Vienna is nearly three hundred miles from here. Foolish letter writing, filled with nonsense, will get you nowhere, and it will cost you your license to collect tolls. Now, stop your impudent talk. Anymore out of you and you will earn ten lashes. And of that, my dear, you can be sure!" Hurriedly, the Count strode through the castle gateway, indignant clouds of misty vapor trailing behind him.

Helena turned and said to Steffan, "Best we begin preparing to defend ourselves, son of my son. Please ask our village elders to meet with us tonight at our house."

CHAPTER EIGHTEEN

That same evening, six village elders sat at the family table, as Helena stood and watched them squabble. She motioned to Maria, and the younger woman served each man another glass of strong, clear peach-flavored *rakia*.

"Good neighbors," Helena interrupted them, holding up her hands to get everyone's attention. "Listen to me. The Turkish leader who led the recent attack promised to return in five years, as you know."

"Tell us again how it is you know this?" one villager asked.

Helena's eyes were bright as she stared at the man, and her face was red with anger. "Women were abused and raped during the raid, as you well know. One was this very woman," she said, putting her arm around Maria's shoulder. "The leader of the raiders took her and her son to one of the storage sheds and threatened to kill my great-grandson if she resisted him."

Every man sitting at the table appeared to be very attentive and avoided looking directly at Maria.

"Afterward, the vain Turk convinced himself that his seed would produce a child from the forced union. Maria is now four months pregnant."

"How do we know she is carrying *his* child?" one man interrupted, glancing at Steffan.

"It is the Turkish commander's, but that makes no difference," Helena said.

"Now, my dear friend, you sound as though you are speculating."

"Wipe that smug smile off your face, Riccardis. Let me tell you exactly what the commanding Turk said, and his threat to all of us."

Maria, who was serving cakes and refilling glasses, stopped in mid-step, and the pottery flask of liquor crashed to the floor. "Oh, Nana," she pleaded.

"Hush, my child, everyone knows about your abuse and that you will give birth in the next few months. What these elders do not know is the Turkish aga's pledge to return in five years, and his threat to all in Kostel." Turning to the men, she continued. "The leader, Aga Abdul Azim, said that if any harm befell *his* child, he would first crucify Maria and her son like Saint Petar, then slay every living person in Kostel, burn everything until the entire fiefdom is a wasteland and cursed for tens of generations. Nothing would remain alive! Therefore, you see, it makes no difference who the actual father is. The opinion of the Turkish leader is all that matters."

No one spoke. The revelation stunned everyone, and there was no restless movement. Only the whisk sound of Maria's broom, sweeping up the pieces of pottery broke the silence.

"Oh, my God in heaven above," Riccardis finally broke the silence.

"May the Good Lord have mercy on us," the man at the end of the table added, burying his head in his hands.

"He said everybody?" Antonio asked.

"That is right—everyone in Kostel."

"Even the children," someone else asked.

Helena nodded.

"Kill every living thing in the fiefdom . . .," Jakob repeated in a whisper.

Again, there were long moments of silence. Then, the villager at the end of the table raised his head. "The path is clear, my friends. The newborn must be cared for by all so that it can be given to the evil Turk when he returns."

Whispering sounds of support arose from the men sitting around the table.

"NEVER," Helena curtly responded, cutting off all the other speakers. "No one is going to take this child from this family! We will not give up the child—and that goes for Maria, Steffan and me. You can rest assured on that point."

"But, be reasonable, Helena, he threatened every . . ."

"No, you are not hearing me, Jakob," she prevailed. "There is more than one way to skin a weasel."

"Wait my neighbors and let us consider the situation," cautioned still another elder. "No one knows for sure that the Turk will return to our village. Maybe God will place other events in his path that will divert him. Helena, you know the old saying, 'Haste is the handmaiden of waste.'"

"Return in five years!" Jakob parroted, still lost in the horror of what might happen to all of them.

Another began, "But, Helena . . . and Maria, too . . . be reasonable . . ." He lapsed into silence under the old woman's withering glower.

Helena stared at each man, in turn, and then spoke more softly. "If necessary, I would rather throw the newborn into the river than offer him as a white slave for the depraved and ungodly Turks and their Ottoman Sultan."

"Helena, you cannot mean that?"

Helena sat down at the kitchen table, as silence engulfed the group once more.

Maria stated her view in a whispered voice, as she wiped her eyes with her white apron. "If it becomes necessary, I am prepared to take the life of my unborn child, along with my own. Never again will I submit to the evil ways of those mongrel *kučkin sins*, bastards!"

The silence was thick, except for a cough.

Helena noticed her son staring at his wife. After long moments, she saw him nod his head. When Steffan glanced her way, she saw the determination on his face and the fire in his eyes. "So, now you know," Helena said, looking at each man seated at the table. "No one in the Klobucar family is going to give up Maria's child to become a white slave for the Turkish Sultan!"

Then, everyone talked at the same time. The discussion, sometimes heated, continued into the night.

Finally, Jakob, seated beside her, said, "So, Helena, you said there is another option. What do you have in mind?"

Helena had remained silent after sitting, her fingers busily embroidering a linen tunic for her new great-grandchild. Laying it aside, she replied, "My longtime neighbors and friends of Am Furtt, it is time for us to stand up to the marauders, after decades of living in the shadow of our fears."

"But, Helena," Riccardis said, "we are poor farmers. We know little about war or tactics. I am afraid you overestimate what we are capable of doing."

"You avoid the question before us, just as the Lord of the Castle does. I confronted Count Erdody today and asked him how he expected to defend us better, during the next Turkish attack. He threatened to have me whipped and berated me in front of the crowd gathered in the marketplace. But not one word was uttered about preparations or plans to protect us or the rest of the fiefdom!"

"You confronted the Lord of Kostel?" Riccardis asked in wide-eyed amazement at her brashness. Then, he asked, "And the Count gave you no answer to your question?"

"That is correct. You can ask Steffan. He was there with me. The man refused to give any assurance that he had a plan, or that he would develop one. Even when I threatened to send a letter to Vienna, complaining about the lack of defenses, he only said I was a foolish old woman and threatened to have me flogged. And our esteemed bishop rose to the Count's defense."

"Helena Klobucar, you threatened the Lord of this Fiefdom with a letter of complaint to Vienna?" the man at the end of the table asked, incredulously.

"That is right. With the man avoiding his responsibility to us, his serfs—the people of Am Furtt have two choices. One is that we can pack our things and leave while trying to find a safer place where we can farm and build a new life. I remind you, though, that we would need Count Erdody's permission to leave this fief. Frankly, that seems unlikely. We know that going south or east places us closer to Muslim raiding parties. If we go north, we will have to travel farther than Gottschee, for the Turkish forces were there six years ago. In fact, the Turks have been as far north as Vienna. So, where is it, exactly, that our people might be safer?"

Again, looking at each of the elders, Helena continued, "The answer is nowhere! Instead, we must draw up a plan to protect ourselves right here!"

The men looked uneasy.

"We have to think about our families and the farms," the man at the end of the table cautioned.

"*Joj*, oh my, and what will you do," Helena said, "when the farms are burned down around your ears. How will any of us survive if that happens?"

"You know we are not warriors," Jakob pleaded.

"I know that well, my dear friend. That is why we must use our heads. The Turks will be confident—overly self-assured—as is always the case. They fully expect no resistance. Finding us prepared—that will be a surprise for them! It will be up to us to take advantage of it."

The discussion continued far into the night, as Maria continued to refill empty glasses.

Steffan had remained quiet throughout the discussion. Finally, he said, "Gentlemen, what option do we have? If it is impractical to leave Kostel, and if the Castle Lord cannot protect us, we have no choice. We must defend ourselves, as best we can. Is there anyone who will argue against the logic of this conclusion?"

All remained quiet and considered what he had said. Then, one elder raised his glass toward Helena, and said, "You have made us open our eyes, Madam Klobucar. You have convictions that are stout like the oak trees in our forests. What would you have us do?"

"We still have plenty of time. Select two from among you. I will join them, and the three of us will draw up a plan. When it is complete, we can meet again to discuss the matter. Is that agreeable to everyone?" Helena asked, looking around the table at each man.

That is how the village of Am Furtt formed a war council.

CHAPTER NINETEEN

Am Furtt
Spring 1581

Easter came late that year. One month earlier, on the twenty-fifth of March, Maria's birthing time arrived. That Thursday began with dark clouds moving across the heavens during the early morning hours, marking the end of a full moon. Old men in the village said the sky indicated that a snowstorm was coming within the next few days. Farm chores were lighter at that time of year, with the work of the *kolinje* behind them, and the cuts of meat hanging and curing in the attic.

Maria arose from her bed to the sound of the cows calling her, dressed and added wood to the central fireplace coals. Suddenly, severe cramps bent her over. *Well, the time is near for my little one,* she thought. *Perhaps, it will come this evening after the day's chores.*

Helena entered the central room and rubbed her hands together over the fireplace flames to warm them. She glanced at Maria, who smiled and nodded to her.

Steffan entered the main room and greeted her, but the air was still frosty between them. Night after night, they lay in the same bed, pretending to sleep until exhaustion finally overtook them, as both listened to Helena snoring. They were courteous to each other, but there were few times when they exchanged a humorous moment or sat next to the fire by themselves. Maria had little idea how Steffan would react to the new baby. They simply did not talk about it, and the silence between them remained tense and awkward. Even so, neither took the first step to close the wound.

Steffan kept busy with work on the farm and preparing for the next Turkish attack. The latter included planning a replacement shed for one that the Turks had burned down. He hoped it would also house a new lethal weapon that he was designing.

Maria began preparing *kaša* for the morning breakfast—ground oats served with cream. Then she laid out pork chops to cook on a grill for the meat course. The mooing of a cow came from the corral. *They are calling, telling me when to rise in the morning and when it is evening,* she thought, smiling to herself.

Helena was busy slicing bread that she had made earlier that morning in bins, baked in a heavy cast iron cooking pot with a lid, next to coals in the fireplace. Setting out butter and lard as spreads for the fresh bread, she placed a pitcher of beer on the table, to complete the preparations for the morning meal, and added a mug of milk for Anton.

After breakfast, Maria left the house, carrying a milk pail. It was only a few steps to the enclosed area adjacent to the house. As she walked, she suddenly paused, as another cramp seized her, doubling her over. Straightening, she continued, walking with her hand on her back. She entered the enclosure, where she drew up her wool tunic and tucked it beneath her belt, exposing the linen undertunic. It was much easier to wash a dirty linen undergarment than one made of wool.

At that time of year, the cow and calf remained in the pen next to the house, as the area received some heat radiating from the central fireplace. No village family would risk losing their milk animals during the cold days of winter. If the weather turned even colder, the cows' safety would become a primary concern. The simple way to solve it was to establish a separate area in the central room of the house and keep the animals inside. The horse, mule, chickens and ducks remained in the barn, located at the rear of the garden, along with the pigpen.

As she continued milking, her thoughts turned back to the day she and Steffan were married. Ceremonies usually took place in the winter months, when farm chores were light, and that was their experience as well. They married in November at the Parish Church of the Blessed Virgin Mary in Fara.

Catholic Church Liturgy strictly forbade intercourse before marriage. Authorities availed themselves of various punishments, including public shaming in stocks, whipping or branding. The most important check, however, was instilling the fear of condemnation as a fornicating sinner, which sentenced a serf to unending purgatory after death, denying the person a place beside Christ in the eternal afterlife.

With the dowry settled, the family negotiators addressed other details. *First,* she recalled, *they introduced Steffan and me formally, and asked each of us if we were willing to marry the other. Given all the gossip we had heard from neighbors, we knew what was coming and had* often thought about it; we were prepared and said "yes." Then, we posted the wedding bands at the parish church in Fara three Sundays before the ceremony. Someone told us that the Castle Lord was advised, and he had no objection, although I have no idea what business it was of his. I guess it is a way for the Church to stay in good graces with the nobility.

We had a rousing celebration following the wedding, which was a happy and noisy occasion, complete with good food and sweets, washed down with vast quantities of beer, wine and rakia. Tambourine musicians from neighboring villages played high-stepping polkas. More than once, we danced the traditional kola. People snaked through the village in a line, holding the shoulder of the person in front with one hand and dancing, first in one direction and then the other; then formed a large circle that eventually coiled smaller until it was tightly interlaced and could move no more.

I dutifully kissed many male hands that day, including those related to my husband, the best man and visitors. By night's end, I was weary from dancing with every man and boy at the celebration. However, Steffan and I were not yet finished, for the priest still had to bless the matrimonial bed—with us in it!

As she pulled on the cow's tit, Maria smiled, remembering the priest's incantation, as she and Steffan tried to control their giggles and remain calm in their nightclothes, with blankets pulled up to their chins. The tipsy priest had downed more than one glass of rakia, but he vainly pretended sobriety.

Father Michael dutifully knelt at the foot of the bed, splashing it, a large area of the floor and us with holy water. I will never forget his prayer as Steffan and I tried to smother our laughter and shake off the water:

Bless, oh Lord, this marriage, and these two people.
May they live in your love and grow old together.
And, with thy guidance, may their souls conjugate
And be rewarded with the birth of many sons.

With her forehead against the cow's warm skin, Maria's smile widened, recalling the following morning when Helena rudely awakened them and shooed both out of bed.

Then, Helena carefully pulled back the blanket and examined the bed sheet. The worry lines on her face turned to a smile, and she hurried out of the house to the waiting throng, holding up the sheet evidencing Maria's chastity.

A tremendous drunken roar arose from the crowd, and the celebration continued for another day. Without the evidence, the Church would have annulled the marriage, and I returned to my parents to live in shame. On the other hand, as I learned much later, Nana Helena probably would have secretly sprinkled red dye on the sheet from a small clay vessel hidden in the pocket of her apron. Maria smiled again and chuckled softly to herself. *She is such a sweetheart.*

She moved into Petar and Helena's farmhouse as was customary. She initially worried about fitting into her new home and life. She enjoyed some status at her parents' farm—not as much as her brother—but she was a respected family member. In the new situation, her position was at the bottom of the ladder, and the family called her *mlada*, their word for "young girl." Her mother provided several pieces of advice on her wedding day: "Abide by orders in your husband's home, with no backtalk. Obey your husband and all elders. Find no faults and pretend to be content." Maria thought she could do these, but her concerns persisted.

She had heard that some brides had to perform menial tasks, such as taking off the family patriarch's muddy boots and washing his feet after a hard day working in the fields. Some *mladas* were required to stand as the family ate meals, holding candles to light the table for others. In other instances, she had heard that husbands beat their brides for not learning the ways of the new household quickly enough. Though such signs of obedience were demeaning, they were not unheard of in Kostelian farming homes.

Later, she learned that Helena had made inquiries before the Klobucars first visit to her parents to begin discussing the dowry. The old woman had talked with priests, then villagers in Vas, as Helena sought a suitable wife for her grandson, someone strong and resilient, who could help guide Steffan and the family with sound advice. The search also seemed to center on finding the right woman to whom she could pass her torch one day, as the family matriarch.

Maria finished milking, then lugged the heavy pail to the house and poured the contents into a large pot hanging from an iron hook over the fire. After boiling the milk and emptying the pot, everyone, young and old, liked to scrape the kettle's sides with their eating knives, savoring the warm residue of cream.

She left to feed the animals in the barn, and she felt a sharp spasm in her back. Walking back to the house, she saw Helena returning from the drying shed.

"I saw your difficulty this morning," Helena said, as she put her arm around the young woman's shoulders. "All is prepared, my daughter," "Do you wish me to be with you when the time comes?"

"Thank you for the kind offer, Nana. Let me go first. Perhaps you can check on me later."

"Very well. Is it time now? Has your water broken?"

"It is not yet time, and my water has not broken. Still, I think I should go to the shed and lie down. Contractions began as I milked the cow this morning." Just as a woman knows when to pull her hand back from a flame, Helena had told her that women innately know when birthing is near.

"Take courage, Maria. The first is always the hardest. I expect your second little one will arrive more quickly."

"That would be a blessing, Nana Helena." Maria walked slowly to the shed, one hand on her waist. She knew from delivering Anton that the pain would hold her in its grasp until she made the final push.

CHAPTER TWENTY

Inside the shed, Maria saw that Helena had laid out a clean sheet on a bed of fodder and in the center was an amulet, honoring Saint Margaret, the virgin patron saint of women giving birth. Slipping the necklace over her head, Maria remembered the saint's tale that Satan, in the form of a dragon, swallowed the woman at the turn of the fourth century and then spat her out, because the wooden crucifix in the woman's hand stuck in the dragon's throat.

There were two pails of clean water near the sheet, several lighted candles, a sharp knife and, as she had requested, a small jug of wine, along with clean clothes for the baby and herself. To one side, two small blankets lay on the bed sheet, including the special one that had welcomed many previous Klobucar babies. Helena's rosary beads lay on top. In one corner of the shed, red-hot coals in a brazier provided warmth.

Dealing with childbirth pain was challenging and dangerous for every mother, and Maria knew that her religious faith played a significant role. Even so, it seemed wise to have familiar things about at such a time, to add spiritual support—the amulet, special birthing blanket and rosary beads.

She removed her wool coat and grimaced again, as the claw of another spasm gripped her, increasing the pain and pressure in her back. She caught her breath until it slowly passed. Looking at the items Helena had prepared, Maria smiled, remembering the surprised expression on Nana Helena's face when she requested adding the small jug of wine along with the other items left in the shed. The older woman did not comment, but the look on her face clearly conveyed her question. *The bastard Turk lectured me on using small quantities. What is there to lose, even if it seems like a pagan practice?*

Suddenly, she cramped, and a series of contractions racked her, each more painful than the previous one. She awkwardly raised her tunic-length hems and got down on her knees, holding onto an upright post for support. Then, slowly and clumsily, she lay down and rolled onto her side, in an attempt to ease the aches. The pressure in her back was severe and continuous, as the contractions came, and then eased, only to return. She rolled onto her other side, seeking one position after another, trying desperately to find one that eased the pains.

Finally, she decided to stand again. Using the big post, she managed to squat on parted knees. Moaning, she pressed her forehead against the rough wood and then, ever so slowly, pulled herself upright. With great care, Maria walked from one side of the shed to the other and then did it again. From time to time, she placed one, or both, hands on her waist or stomach, trying various positions that lessened the sharp stabs and eased the relentless pressure in her back.

She walked for a long time. During one of her easier periods, she ran her fingers over her distended abdomen and smiled, as she felt her inverted navel. Without warning, severe pain caused her to stop abruptly. Easing her way to the pillar again, she grasped it and bent down, then stretched one leg after the other, as she sought relief. She felt a soft pop and warm liquid ran down her legs. *At last, it comes,* she noted, grimacing.

She bore down hard, as the next contraction gripped her. Instinctively, she realized that she must get down to a squatting position, and used the post once more for support, her legs trembling with the exertion of lowering herself to a kneeling position.

Then, the contractions came in waves that she rode, from high pressure and pain down into valleys of exhaustion and weakness. Straining and moaning loudly, she pushed hard. Clenching her teeth, she pushed again. One hand held onto a sidewall slat in a death-like grip to steady herself, and her other hand was between her legs, feeling the baby's head, as the youngster began to push through.

Suddenly, she screamed in excruciating pain. She swayed slowly, steadying herself with her handhold on the side slat. Clumsily, she rested on one knee, then the other, and finally, she was on her hands and knees. Again, the contractions came, and these were ever more powerful. Placing her right hand between her legs, she felt the baby's head again. Slowly, she maneuvered herself into a squatting position, with her back against the post. A priest had told her weeks earlier that birthing pains for women were the ongoing reminders of the original sin committed by Adam and Eve. *Ha, easy for him to say,* she had thought at the time; *he is a man who likely flinches when his finger catches a wood sliver, much less the pain of giving birth to a baby with a big head, two shoulders and a rump.* 'So, answer me one question,' she had asked him: 'What on-going pain do men have from the same original sin?' His answer was that 'men were doomed to hard labor for their entire lifetime.'

At the time, it had sounded like a contrived explanation; now, given the pains of birthing, it seemed simplistic and almost comical.

"Come, my darling!" she called to the youngster that was trying to make its way into the world. "Come to me, precious one. *Coooommmmm!*" she screamed, then clenched her teeth while arching her back into a nearly impossible position. She gasped for breath, tightly closing her eyes. "Push hard," she screamed to herself, as another contraction overtook her. The pressure in her head and against the back of her eyelids was like the hammering sounds of a heavy mallet beating against a blacksmith's anvil. Then, she felt the little one's shoulders wiggle through, one by one. Gritting her teeth, she gave a final push as the muscles of her body released, and the infant came out in a rush while her hands protected and guided the newborn onto the coverlet. It was a large bundle.

Maria untangled the cord and lifted the baby, tears of joy streaming down her cheeks. "Well, Mathias, you Turkish bastard," she said, "you have your first son—Rado." Suddenly, the horrific pains eased, and she smiled at the red, wrinkled face of her newborn child.

Gently, she cleaned his mouth, nose and eyes with a cloth and water. The baby responded with a loud scream, screwed up his eyes into an impossible squint and his red face contorted into a mask of infant fury. Tiny arms flailed, and one leg kicked out as the boy squirmed in his new world. Nana had provided wool thread, and Maria tied the umbilical cord off near the baby's stomach and then severed it. Finally, she placed a drop of wine on the end and bound it with a narrow linen cloth, which she wound around the baby. A moment later, Maria expelled the afterbirth.

From afar, she heard the shed door open, and she looked up to see Helena entering.

"Come see your new great-grandson, Nana Helena. I have named him Rado."

"*Bog blagosloviti,* God bless! Let me hold the newest member of our family for just a moment." Then, looking at Maria, there was a puzzled expression on Helena's face. "That sounds like the name the barbarian asked you to . . ." The old woman stopped, looking at her quizzically. She did not finish, but asked, "Am I right?"

"Yes, I decided that I liked it. It is like a short version of our Christian name, Radovoy." Watching through tearful eyes, Maria saw love on the old woman's face.

"*Joj,* oh my, he is beautiful. He looks like his mother. We must quickly have him baptized, hopefully tomorrow. While he is newborn, he has not sinned. Yet, church doctrine says he carries the original sin of Adam and Eve until baptism takes place. God forbid that he should die beforehand, eternally denying his immortal soul entry into heaven. Tomorrow," she said firmly, "we will take him to the priest." She freed Maria's breast from the tunic, gave a light squeeze to begin the milk, then raised the baby for his first suckling.

First putting a drop of wine on her finger, Maria rubbed her swollen nipple. She knew that Helena watched her with an odd expression on her face. Still, if such a simple thing would better assure her baby's survival, it was a welcome addition to the birthing tradition.

Hungrily, the infant suckled her breast.

The two women were simultaneously smiling and crying, as Rado noisily fed.

Looking at Maria, Helena said, "We must wrap him in the special birthing blanket. The priests say that such practices are nonsense, but you listen to your Nana. He is still in danger of dying from the strange things that affect newborns. Tomorrow, after the baptism in Fara, we will make a pilgrimage to the Chapel of the Holy Three Kings in Market Kostel, and we will say a special prayer for him. What last name do you wish to use for the boy?"

The question stumped Maria. Then, she replied, "Would it offend the family if it was Klobucar, Nana? I do not know how Steffan feels about this, as we have never discussed it."

"It is a fine name for the boy. If anyone's nose bends out of shape, I will straighten it for them. Steffan will come around. You will see." Looking and smiling at the tiny wondrous miracle of new birth, she added, "No one is going to take this baby from us."

"I know," Maria answered. "No one is going to steal my son, no matter what happens!"

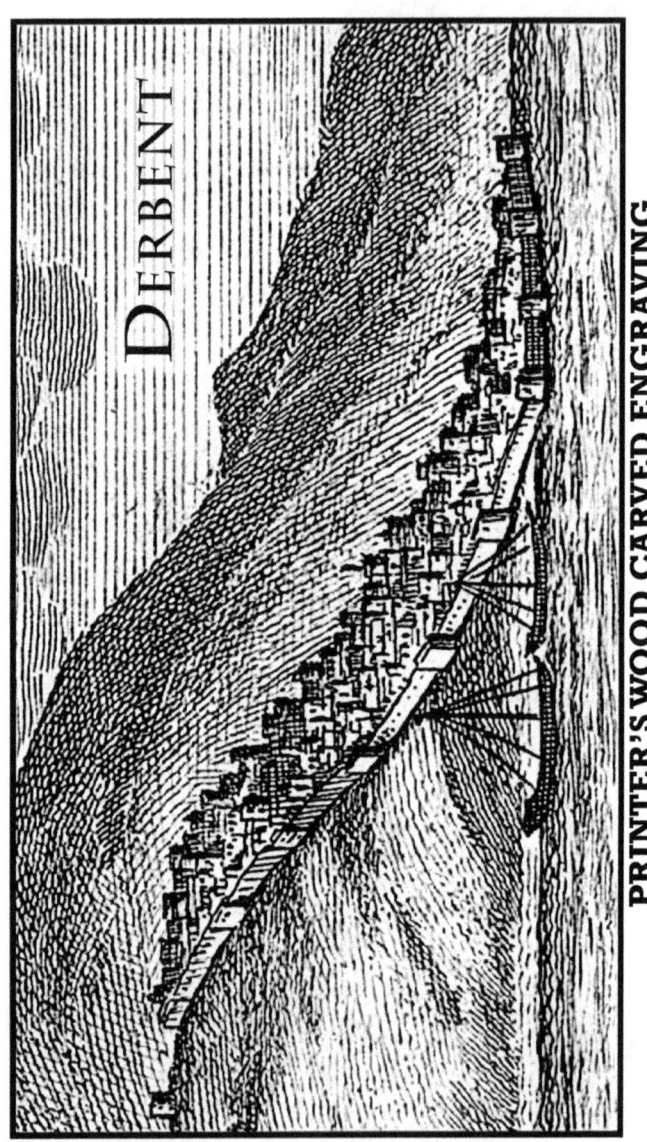

PRINTER'S WOOD CARVED ENGRAVING

Book II
Battle of Torches
Caspian Sea
1583

CHAPTER TWENTY-ONE

May 8, 1583

From a hilltop ridge, Aga Abdul Azim gazed at the broad panorama spread before him, as a light breeze tugged at his tall, white-crowned Janissary hat and his flowing tunic. Even from that distance, he stared in awe at the colossal fortress and the sheer size and length of the massive structure, lying on the plain next to the Caspian Sea.

It took unbelievable toil and workmanship for slaves to construct those great walls, he marveled, *and likely over an extended period of time—probably centuries before fully encircling the city of Derbent, the "locked gate," or "gate of gates," and its sixty thousand inhabitants. Some even referred to the fortress as the "Gates of Alexander," despite the lack of evidence that the famed general and his army had come that way.*

Before leaving on the Derbent campaign, he had visited the Istanbul's vaults and archives of documents to learn more about the city-fortress and its history. Some historians speculated that the first occupation occurred more than one thousand years earlier and that the fortress may have originally begun as a defense against nomadic raiders from the north. From his visit, he recalled that one sage writer provided the following description:

> It undulates over the slopes like an enormous boa,
> Sprawling down the mountains
> With sunlight roofs as scales,
> And the elevated head rises as a tooted head,
> While the serpent's tail plays in the Caspian Sea.

The fortress comprised two walls that ran west to east, parallel to each other, for nearly one and one-half miles—on a bench of land that extended from steep mountain foothills to the blue waters of the sea. Azim's eye gauged the inside distance between the walls at about one thousand yards.

Exterior walls consisted of inner and outer skins of shaped stone blocks. Rocks, dirt and debris filled the interior space, creating a thickness of ten feet at the base. The defensive structure followed the contours of the steeply undulating terrain, down-sloped to the sea. Additional stone fortifications squared the parallel walls at each end to complete the stronghold's rectangular shape. Lastly, an amazing seventy-three square or barrel-vaulted watchtowers were strategically interspersed along the perimeter, rising more than sixty feet high that overlooked the thirty-foot walls and surrounding terrain.

Spies informed him that fourteen portals had once pierced the twin walls of the fortress. As news of the advancing Ottoman Army reached Derbent, the Persians took defensive measures and walled in half with stone blocks. The gates of the remaining portals were framed with heavy timber, then cross-ribbed with thick logs and sheathed in bronze, to resist damage from battering rams and fire.

Our modern siege guns will deal harshly with those walls, Azim concluded. *Yet, it is a daunting task that our commanders are undertaking, expecting to complete the submission of this vast fortress within three days. I know our Army is practiced and disciplined but is such a goal really possible? Well, we shall see.*

Inside the fortress, he saw that the defenders were prepared to respond with large ballistas—weapons resembling giant torsion-operated crossbows that hurled casks of gunpowder or large arrows—pointed south toward the Turkish forces. Azim involuntarily shuddered at the thought of men who would be at the receiving end of such lethal barrages.

Two days earlier, he had journeyed to the eastern end of the fortress and was amazed to find that the cut-and-shaped block walls extended into the sea for some five hundred yards. Then, the wall turned to square off the end, which provided sheltered moorage within for single-sail ships, known as *dhows,* that plied the Caspian, moving goods, travelers—and pirates. To prevent surprise attacks from the sea, he learned that the Persians stretched a log boom across the opening every evening.

During journeys as an Ottoman warrior, I have seen many impressive architectural wonders. Some of my favorites is the Sultan's magnificent Topkapi Palace, splendidly sprawling over hundreds of acres in a minaret-filled skyline. A close second is the ornately and hauntingly beautiful Hagia Sofia, which was the most important Christian cathedral in the world for one thousand years, only to continue its venerated use as an Islamic mosque, following the fall of the largest city in Europe to we Turks in 1453. Both of these are located in Istanbul. Also in my travels, I have marveled at the ostentatiously imposing columns and soaring roofline of the ancient Pentium, sitting high above Athens, and the impressively fortified seaport city-state of Dubrovnik. Yet, none has given me the same ominous feeling as this fortress city, snaking down the narrow offset of land.*

He swept off his tall hat and wiped the sweat from his brow with the sleeve of his flowing red and yellow caftan. Even in the early morning, the day was warm. A man on the Pasha General's staff told him that the temperature was typical and that the region received minimal rainfall during the first five months of the year. The weather was a key factor in establishing the timing of the Ottoman battle plan to retake Derbent.

Geographical location plays such an important role in fortifications, Azim mused. *That is certainly true for this narrow plain below me. To the east, the horizon fills with the blue waters of the Caspian Sea, extending as far as my eyes can see. Westward, a smaller chain of mountains begins the seven hundred mile range of the Caucasus Mountains. That spine of icy peaks extends from here to the Black Sea— except for this narrow stretch of land.*

Through the centuries, scholars say emperors, kings, sultans, brigands and warlords fought to control the fortress and this stretch of land. They collected tolls from travelers for the right to pass north or south through the city, over a route that intersected with the ancient Silk Roads traveling from lands so distant beyond the eastern horizon that half-years measure progress and journey time.

Traders have a choice, Azim noted—*pass through this fortress and pay the toll, or sail around it by ship and risk losing cargo and their lives to pirating brigands plying the Caspian.*

Water was the lifeblood for any fortress, and critical in a dry climate. Azim knew that the water reserves lay beneath an eleven-acre sub-fortress named the *Naryn-Kala,* located at the western end of the stronghold. Originally, this part of Derbent was the palace compound and sat at the highest elevation within the citadel, overlooking the rest of the city.

Beyond the *Naryn-Kala* and western end cap, a single wall, also thirty feet tall, continued up the grass-covered slopes and disappeared out of view into the hillside tree line. Local shepherds reported that it continued up the mountain, over a tortuous twisting landscape, and then along a sharp spiny ridge, until ending at the base of an escarpment located twenty miles to the west. Along that single wall, periodic watchtowers afforded broad sweeping views for lookouts, and when lighted with signal fires, these provided warnings to the main fortress of approaching danger.

Azim's five-hundred soldiers would begin marching to the west tomorrow at the same time that Ottoman cannons, catapults and siege guns commenced firing. The objective of his troop was to launch a surprise attack on the third day of the battle. The single wall atop the spiny ridge would guide them out of the mountains and down to the main fortress while morning darkness concealed their movements—at least, that was the plan.

We have our work cut out for us, and much will be done in the dark. Then, when we reach the fort, we will have a wide area to spread out for our attack, along the high walkways of the walls, he thought, as a heightened sense of anticipation stirred within him. He knew that the *Naryn-Kala* contained the ancient parts of the city as well as the *Dag-Bary*, the "Mountain Wall Gate" at the fortress's southwest corner—the closest to the mountain slopes. That entryway was the primary target for Azim's troops.

CHAPTER TWENTY-TWO

Still enraptured with his view, Azim's attention turned toward the whole Ottoman Army that also spread out before him. *Fifty thousand men plus equipment, animals, siege towers, cannons and supplies are encamped on the plain and stretch as far as I can see. By all that is holy, this is a sight few men will ever come across in their lifetime,* Azim thought.

There are untold cooking pots down there, hanging from iron tripods over campfires. The smoke, combined with dust created by thousands of soldiers and an even greater number of animals, raises a dense cloud in the sky, which hangs permanently over the staging area—as men wait and prepare for the fight to begin. Should Allah grant that I live to be one hundred years old, never again could I expect to see such a magnificent sight!

A convoy of ships sailed from Istanbul through the Bosporus Straits and then eastward along the southern waters of the Black Sea, carrying artillery pieces and heavy munitions—indeed, the entire army—to the city of Trabzon. This deep-water port was founded as a trading colony in the 8th century BC, and it was one of the western destinations on the fabled Silk Road, trafficking in a vast array of goods, such as textiles, carpets, paper, herbs, spices, horses, silver and, particularly, silk. Over the centuries, various conquerors had captured the city until the late 15th century, when it became a provincial capital of the Ottoman Empire.

Azim always marveled at the organization and exacting task involved in transporting and sustaining fifty thousand men. Troops, horses, camels, equipment, food, arrows, guns, ammunition and the supplies needed to maintain the large fighting force—all traveled the same route.

From the docks, all the military equipment and the army, including Azim and his troops, made the difficult, five-hundred-mile eastward trek. The journey took them between the majestically soaring, glacier-covered peaks of the Caucasus Mountains to the north and the twin, glacier-capped summits of Mount Ararat to the south, the final legendary resting place of Noah's ark, as cited in the *Book of Genesis*. Reaching the banks of the Caspian Sea, the Ottoman Army turned northward toward the city and walls of Derbent, after a march of eight months.

From his hilltop location, he saw the Anatolia cavalry corps in the middle of the Turkish line, with its dark red banners waving in the air, each adorned with three white crescents. These were part of Haydar Pasha's forces. Corrals behind their encampment contained the two-hump Bactrian camels, and he figured there must be at least two thousand fighters in the troop.

He had once served in such a unit and was knowledgeable about the animals, equipment and tactics. *Mature camels weigh up to one ton and stand six to seven feet at the shoulder. They are capable of withstanding harsh conditions with a high tolerance for cold temperatures and can lose nearly twenty-five percent of their body weight in hot weather. While their urine is thick, the animal's feces are dry and immediately usable in a campfire. These animals typically live as long as a man does—forty to fifty years.*

When charging the enemy, a mature camel was fast, reaching speeds of forty miles an hour in short bursts, or a sustained pace of twenty-five miles per hour. For control, a rider held a single line attached to the animal's muzzle. Alternatively, the animal was capable of carrying a load of up to one thousand pounds, depending on its physical size.

To the left of that corps, he saw a long horse trap running parallel to the fort's southern wall. It comprised two wide trenches, fitted along the bottoms with sharpened wooden stakes. Behind the traps, there were thousands upon thousands of archers and, beyond on a broad ridge, hundreds of cannons.

Then, there was *Great Turkish Bombard*. From Azim's studies at the Istanbul archives, he learned more about the largest Ottoman siege gun ever built. It, too, was here for the Derbent campaign. Transporting the massive cannon and its supplies was challenging. It required sixty oxen to pull the lead wagon. The gun comprised two long bronze sections to facilitate transport, which screwed together to form a single gun barrel. A dedicated squadron of four thousand men attended it.

He knew it was positioned well back from the other fighting units; in fact, it was out of sight, given its long firing range. The gigantic, seventeen-foot-long cannon weighed nearly twenty tons and had a forty-two-inch barrel. It shot stone balls, which were over two feet in diameter and weighed fifteen hundred pounds, at targets that were up to four thousand yards away. With the wheels removed, cannoneers drove wedges into the ground, which provided minor aiming and elevation changes. These small corrections, coupled with the muzzle-loaded weapon's long range, permitted the big monster to cover a broad sweep of targets. When the gun fired, anyone within miles—in all directions— felt the ground tremble and heard the thunderous detonation, as echoes rebounded off the foothills and across the land, the sound finally rolling out to sea and dissipating. Army officials gave precautionary warnings for local pregnant women to stay indoors during the fighting and advised mothers to stuff the ears of younger children.

Despite his research, Azim was astonished at the size of the weapon. *It looked evil, despite its outlandishly red-painted décor, which they say burns off at the first firing. Still, our Turkish artillery commanders are genuinely concerned that the build-up of intense heat from each firing may split or warp the gun barrel. Consequently—and amazingly—the monster shoots only three times a day. During the intervening time, cannoneers cool the metal with olive oil.*

Twenty thousand archers would begin firing their massed flights of arrows to signal the start of the attack on the third morning. Near their firing positions, enormous wooden barrels held mountainous quantities of arrows, while the soldiers' battle shields were stacked nearby, in an orderly manner. When the siege guns finally breached the walls, these same archers formed into infantry companies, armed with muskets, spears, and *yatagans*. Their banners and shields carried an image of an arrow running through a gold crescent, set against a dark green background.

Azim saw many red or green pennants fluttering in the light breeze while some ensigns were nothing more than horsetails hanging from tall poles. Gold edging appeared on many flags, marking regimental insignias; all contained crescent symbols outlined in white or gold. Like the archers, the metal shields of these soldiers were stuck in the ground for temporary storage, standing row after row, like silent witnesses to the coming battle, carrying the same themes and colors as the banners. Irregular troops in flowing robes and caftans also carpeted the area, adding to the vivid array of clothing, chain mail, tents, equipment, supplies, and animals.

On the third day of the battle, the ten thousand Janissaries were to be the point of the spear in the attack on the Persian stronghold. They would move into action after Azim's troops threw open the Mountain Wall Gate, adding their fighting prowess as a surprise flanking attack from the *Naryn-Kala* end of the fortress. Azim noted the white, distinctive headgear of the Janissary Corps camped below his location.

Parked gun wagons were on the far left of the plain. These carried mobile troops, riding in heavily constructed vehicles and pulled by large, armored draft horses. He smiled recalling the effectiveness of these wagons. *They allow our commanders to react to changing enemy tactics and deliver archers and soldiers swiftly to breaches in defensive walls, or where needed on the battlefield. The army adopted this useful tactic after bitter lessons learned from earlier wars with the Hungarians.*

At the foot of his observation hill, artillery batteries lined the ridges. Each grouping consisted of several cannons targeting a designated section of the fortress wall. Over the course of many sieges and wars, the Turkish Army had found that repeated bombardment of the same three points on a fortress wall—two high and one low in the middle—was the quickest way to reduce stone walls to rubble.

The military musicians made their camp at the rear of the encampment. Azim smiled at seeing them. Such groups were a part of any large military force these days.

For some weeks, these men, and others chanted religious versus, played their flutes, cymbals, horns and drums while walking outside the fortress walls. The cacophony of music and chants is a campaign tactic, devised a century earlier, and used to unnerve the waiting enemy within the fort. I hope it works, but I have always had my doubts about how effective they are.

Scanning the tops of the fortress' walls, Azim's experienced eye noted the solid and notched crenellations, alternating with open spaces and embrasures every several feet. Each set sheltered at least two defenders along the battlement and parapet walkways. It allowed one archer to let loose his arrow, followed immediately by another, as the soldiers continued a steady rain of death on men attacking from below. The same was true for the musketeers, although firing and reloading times averaged four minutes, and their range was no greater than that of a good archer.

It is likely that some of us will be fighting along those high walkways in a few days, Azim reflected. *I pray Allah looks favorably on our task and rewards our deeds.*

Thinking back to his preparatory studies in Istanbul, he concluded, *I believe the historian I read describing Derbent had it right. This fort does look like an evil reptile—one with armored sides that snap and spit deadly fire.*

CHAPTER TWENTY-THREE

Azim sat in the warm sun with his back against a large stone, eyes closed. For the moment, he was lost in his thoughts. It had been several years since his journey to the Kupa Valley, yet the memory of Maria, in the village of Am Furtt, continued to revisit him. He vividly recalled how he had made the threat to return and destroy Kostel if she disobeyed him about their newly conceived child.

He also remembered storming out of the shed and, at the time, never expected to see Kostel or the peasant woman again. After all, who could foretell the future? Even so, he never forgot her and their lovemaking. It was as though she had entered his being—his very soul—and nothing erased those memories from his mind. At night, he found himself dreaming about her. Images of her svelte, full-breasted figure filled his head, as did her dark hair and blazing blue eyes.

The mental pictures of her standing in a ray of sunlight, turning around at his command, her rounded buttocks giving way to the dark-haired valley between her thighs, captured his mind's eye as well as his desire for fulfillment that only she could provide. Despite the intervening years, he was as captivated now with Maria Klobucar as he had been then.

"Good day to you, Aga," Tasar called to him, walking toward him.

Irritated at the interruption, Azim kept the annoyance off his face and remained calm. Inwardly sighing and placing the memories of Maria in a secret place at the back of his mind, he waved a welcome to his barrel-chested second in command. Azim also had another second officer now, named Srdoc, who had joined his unit months earlier before leaving Istanbul.

Tasar looked perplexed, sitting down next to him and leaning back against the same stone. "Aga, our army captured Derbent five years ago," Tasar began, "then lost it. How could such a thing have occurred, given the fortification we see below us?"

"It is quite easy to explain," Azim replied. "We drew back too many soldiers to Istanbul and left an insufficient force for such a massive fortification. The Persians continued their hit and run attacks for years, then blockaded the port and the fort's gates. Our appointed governor confronted two choices: Our garrison could either smash through the Persian line and survive or stay in Derbent and starve to death. Using all the troops at his command, they created a wedge, drove through the enemy and took refuge in the *Darial Gorge* of the Caucasus Mountains, west of here. With its steep terrain, that location was readily defensible, and thus they survived."

"It is odd that the fort has so many watchtowers along the walls, Aga. What do you think?"

"In more peaceful times, this area is renowned for its carpet making, particularly those using silk thread. After the carpet is finished and washed, it is hung on the outside of a tower to cure and dry."

Tazar gave him a perplexed look. "Really? They hang hand-woven carpets from the tops of the tall towers?"

"Yes."

"Further, the towers provide excellent visibility of military actions in all directions. The Persians also use them to communicate within the fort. Our spies tell us that each section of the outer walls has a color assigned to it. By raising and lowering pennants, commanders can move their Persian forces from one area to another.

"The large size of the city and fort stagger the senses, yet the bench of land here is narrow. By Allah, it is an excellent place to collect tolls from passing caravans," Tasar added, his face expressing obvious admiration for man's ingenuity in exercising his greed.

"True enough. Some say that building the fortress began one thousand years ago, to control travel along this segment of the Silk Road, where trade occurs between the Eurasian Steppes to the north and the dry arid lands southward. The Caucasus Mountains are, indeed, an intimidating obstacle for travelers. Scholars describe the steep recesses and soaring peaks as resembling pillars, which hold up the blue heavens and stretch from one horizon to another between the Caspian and the Black seas. They are the most effective walls Allah could create. Recall the months it took for us to travel the southern flank of those mountains."

"No wonder we have raised such a large army to recapture this fort from the Persians," Tasar marveled. "I hope we have enough men and guns. To defeat them, we must reckon with this immense fortification. Not an enviable task, Aga, especially since our troops will have to climb steep slopes just to reach the base of those fearful walls! The Persian archers will have a field day shooting downward at our men."

"Quite right, Tasar! But, that is what our soldiers do—attack the enemy, no matter how difficult."

"Too bad there is not another way."

Azim shrugged and continued with his narrative. "As you know, Osman Pasha commands the forces to the left, including our Janissary Corps, while Cafer Pasha and Haydar Pasha do the same in the center and the other flank. Our commanders say that there are sixty thousand Persian defenders inside the fortress, including a host of Georgian irregulars, and all under the command of Imam Kulu."

"Considering the number of soldiers and the massive fortress walls," Tasar observed, "it will be a real challenge for our army."

"With the Prophet's guidance, we will take it again. Yes, they have thick walls, but we are mobile, and that may prove their undoing. Tasar, I want some of your men to draw a detailed map of the western portion of the fort, which the Persians call *Naryn-Kala*. You see it there at the end of the fortress, separated by the interior curtain wall," Azim pointed with his swagger stick. "We will use the map to brief all the men tomorrow evening and assign them duties after we reach the main fort. It is critical for our secret task that the men know and memorize the details. Our brothers in arms begin their bombardment attack tomorrow. We are to strike in the dark hours of early morning on the third day. After we overpower the defenders guarding the *Naryn-Kala*, we will continue through the city's lanes and alleys toward the sea until we join up with our brothers attacking the other end of the fortress."

Pointing again, Azim continued, "Pay particular attention to the gate that is nearest to the foothills in the *Naryn-Kala*. In Persian, the name means the "Mountain Wall Gate." It is our primary target, and we must capture it and throw it open, allowing our division of ten thousand Janissary brothers waiting on the outside to swarm through like the flooding waters of a Bosporus tide. Our large force will attack the Persian's flank while it is still dark. It should come as quite a surprise for them. But nothing happens without us opening that gate."

Tasar turned to stare at the portal. "It is good that we do not have to deal with an additional portcullis sliding outside the massive entry door." Analyzing the situation, he added, "The tower above the entrance must be at least sixty feet high! We will have to capture and hold it."

Nodding, Azim replied, "We will lead our men around the lower-lying foothills tomorrow and then west along the base of the mountain range. On the second day, we will climb to the singular wall at the top of the mountains and use it to guide us back to the main fortification in the dark for the surprise attack."

"When we reach the top of the wall, how far will it be to the main fort?"

"It is unclear. Our commanders estimate that it is ten to twelve miles, depending on how straight they built this part of the fortification. Our plan allows us two days to reach the walls of the main fortress. In the meantime, bombardments by the big guns and catapults will hammer the eastern end to breach the walls. Then, our irregular troops will engage the defenders, and they will be the first to bloody the Persians. There is no sense wasting experienced and trained Ottoman fighting men to make the initial contact when we have so many irregulars who have joined us seeking adventure and plunder. The regular regimental cavalry will follow and attack the second day."

His new man, Josephus Srdoc, joined them and heard the last few comments. The expression on his face and his shifting eyes were the only evidence of the man's excitement at the thought of the upcoming battle. "By all that is holy," Srdoc noted, "the plan is truly ambitious. Our Pasha generals expect to take this magnificent fort and defeat sixty thousand defenders—and all within three days! That will indeed be quite a feat for our Army if Allah wills it!"

Tasar added, "If it gets too grim for the Persians, they can always throw open the gates on the other side of the fort and flee the city to the north."

Srdoc smiled at the thought.

Azim nodded. He had asked others about his new man's capability before leaving Istanbul, and Srdoc generally received high marks for bravery and battle experience. Even so, some said he had a low boiling point and tended to lose his temper quickly.

Srdoc was tall, well over six feet, with broad shoulders, although not as barrel-chested as Tasar. When aroused, his deep-set green eyes carried a particular glint of rebelliousness. His most distinctive feature was the sword scar that ran down the left cheek of his face, from the edge of his eye to the corner of his lip. The end of the scar permanently puckered his mouth to one side, giving him a look of scorn. Even worse, it turned Srdoc's facial expression into a menacing mask when the man smiled.

Azim had noticed that Srdoc seemed to display an attitude of superiority when walking, holding himself ramrod straight, with a lofty bearing. More than once, Azim observed his high spirits for anything having to do with fighting and killing.

Since arriving in the Derbent area, Azim and his officers drilled their troops through a range of exercises, training them specifically for their unique assignment. Climbing ropes, hand-over-hand, with full loads on their backs was one. In other drills, the troopers practiced navigating at night by the stars. They also practiced connecting and using long ladders in the dark. All were part of refreshing their skills for this particular undertaking.

Tasar continued, "The men are drilled, and I believe they are ready."

"Thank you for the efforts that you have both shown," Azim commented. "However, it will be worthless if we do not accomplish our part of the attack—and throw open the Mountain Wall Gate."

"I am fascinated by the Greek firebombs, Aga," Srdoc added. "They should make quite a blaze within the fortress."

During the many weeks of preparation, their troopers made over one thousand Greek firebombs. Azim's men pressed every potter in the region into making the small-sized clay containers, while Azim and his officers supervised. Other soldiers oversaw the distillation of the black, volatile muck that oozed out of the ground south of Derbent. The odor was overpowering and repugnant, but the nauseating black mixture also had unusually valuable properties in wartime. It was exceedingly flammable and attempting to extinguish it with water served only to spread the flames.

Azim's troopers added six-inch fuses to each pot after filling the clay flasks. Then, they packed each vessel in leather satchels using straw for cushioning. Camels would transport the load until they reached the single wall, high in the mountains. At that point, the Janissaries would shoulder the bags on their backs.

CHAPTER TWENTY-FOUR

Day One
May 9

The Turkish bombardment against the fort began, and Azim's soldiers broke camp before dawn and marched westward. Behind them, they heard and felt the tremendous artillery shock waves of Turkish cannons firing on Derbent and its fortress walls.

Azim's force camped that afternoon in a hollow, well hidden away from a casual traveler or wandering shepherd. He and his lieutenants divided the large troop between them and drilled the men on specific assignments. They took turns reviewing the map Tasar's men had sketched. All pointed out the Mountain Wall Gate and conveyed every scrap of information they had on the *Naryn-Kala* area of the fort.

Day Two
May 10

Azim's special troops began climbing the mountain early the next morning. The company took great care to remain off ridges and to avoid becoming silhouettes against the landscape. They used the natural terrain and paralleling canyons. Nerves were taut, as they followed beaten animal trails along the contours of hillsides, slowly winding higher. Frustratingly, they encountered several blind canyons or steep-walled gorges that were too risky and challenging for the men and camels. Then, they had to turn back and try a different route to continue their climb. Azim had hired two young, local goat herders that morning as guides to avoid these very problems. The two claimed to know the mountains well.

After the column had reversed itself for the third time, Azim called the two herders to where he stood, apart from his men. Backtracking on the trail wasted time and energy, and he knew that Srdoc was ready to tear the two teenagers apart. All his lieutenant needed was a sign from him.

With a nod from Azim, Srdoc joined them. Menacingly, his second rubbed the shiny streak of scar tissue running down the side of his face, breaking into his evil looking version of a smile. The two youngsters drew back, terrorized by the presence of his second in command.

Aga Azim grabbed the folds of each boy's tunic and brought their heads together until the three were close and almost touching. Srdoc slipped inside the circle as well to the obvious distress of the two boys who involuntarily stiffened.

In a calm voice, Azim said, "These are impressive heights, boys, and it would be easy to exhaust my men long before we reach the summit. How is it that we continue to run into so many difficulties, considering your knowledge of these mountains?"

The oldest answered first. "Aga, there are so many hills and valleys that we become confused. Allah be praised, it happens, you know."

Azim looked at the younger boy, his anger rising, but outwardly, he remained calm.

The youngster was looking down and creating little round circles in the dirt with his big toe.

"And besides," the oldest continued, "we almost never come this far west with our goat herds."

Azim pondered the response for a moment. The fearful expression on his face clearly showed his disbelief, as he furtively glanced sideways at Srdoc. Then, shifting his grip to the backs of the boys' necks, he replied to the eldest, "Should it occur just one more time, I shall be obliged to cut off your manhood!"

Both youngsters stiffened at the threat and sought to pull away, but Azim's hold on their necks was unshakable.

Azim continued, again in a soft, but firm voice. "And then, I will feed them to your cousin here," he said, as his hard gaze moved to the younger boy. "And if you also fail me, I shall have Srdoc roll both of your heads down the mountain, so my men can wager which will travel the farthest." Switching his penetrating gaze to the older boy again, Azim added, "You know, Allah be praised, it happens!"

The teenagers looked at him, their eyes wild with fear. Both aggressively nodded their understanding. "It will be as you say, and my cousin and I will be most careful," the eldest said. His cousin continued to draw lines in the dirt, only now with greater vigor.

"I hope my meaning is perfectly clear to the two of you. I hired you to help us locate the best routes. May I strongly suggest that you both set your minds to the task and get on with it, for we have no more time to waste on trails that lead nowhere. One of you should scout ahead to avoid any more blind canyons. Now, are there any questions?" he asked, releasing his grip on their necks.

"No, sir . . . I mean, yes sir, Aga," the oldest goat herder stammered, bowing and backing away. "We understand you perfectly and will do as you request." With that, the two turned and scampered away.

"Srdoc," Azim said, "see that our two guides do not lead us astray again. If necessary, deal with them firmly and finally."

With a wicked gleam in his eyes, his second nodded. "It will be done as you say, Aga."

There were no more false trails, as the party slowly continued toward the towering summit. The setting sun cast elongated shadows on the mountain's hollows and ravines, as Azim's five-hundred troops and two hundred camels slowly made their way up the tortuous slopes toward the high cliffs. In some areas, tree branches entirely roofed swales with their leafy canopy, creating an artificial darkness, as though the sun had already set and the moonless night had begun.

More than once, they had to scale steep slopes and lower braided ropes, which were strong enough to assist the heavily loaded pack animals up the sides. It was slow, backbreaking work. Azim felt fortunate that he had such a large number of troopers to help with all the heavy work. As they rested for the final time, Azim had the men break out food and water. They had packed their heavier clothes, knowing that the higher elevation and nightfall would bring much colder temperatures.

He sat looking at the magnificent view to the south and caught sight of the lower portion of the Caspian Sea to the east. The blue water reminded him of Maria's eyes, and his mind drifted to memories of the past.

Does my son resemble me, Azim wondered? I know his name is Rado, for surely I did not sire a daughter. I must return and claim that which is mine. By the end of this battle, it will be almost time to think about returning for another journey to Kostel for devsirme.

His mind continued to wander. Meticulously, he recounted and dwelt on his lovemaking with Maria, trying to recapture every detail. He vividly recalled her figure and every facial feature, the image of her naked body on the soft pallet, tantalizingly beautiful with her long, dark hair, as they lay in the storage shed; their bodies conformed together, as though a sculptor had cast them as a single statue of bronze. He remembered that she had whimpered softly at one point, and he had felt her heart beating under his hand.

Some memories had become less clear in his mind over time such as the bitter final words between them, but the startling color of her eyes was indelible. He also recalled her swollen nipples from nursing, jutting from the darker, blood red areola. *I wonder if that man of hers, or someone else, arouses her these days as I did. Perhaps, when she lies with her dull, peasant husband, she thinks favorably of our time together—and me. I will wager that she has not had the same womanly release since our time together. I know their Christian religion, and it is far too inhibiting. Their strict religious orthodoxy inhibits many pleasures that are the essence of life itself.*

His most worrisome thoughts were about the child, born from his coupling with Maria. He had no doubt that conception had taken place despite the lack of any facts. Azim was supremely confident in this regard although there was no logical explanation. Still, he also recognized that the odds of the boy surviving were questionable—details that Maria had made very clear to him. *There is only one way to know, and that will be to return to Am Furtt in a few years—if I survive this war.*

Ominously, an expression of anger showed on his face. *No one, and I mean no one, had better harm Rado, for I will raise the boy in Istanbul to become a great Janissary warrior, like his sire!*

During the Army's stop to unload war materials in Trabzon, Azim and Tasar had free time. Late one afternoon after prayers, they had visited a coffee house in the grand bazaar, where musicians had played, and the familiar smells of tobacco smoke and burning incense had mingled and wafted in the air. The room had been full of men, most of whom were drawing smoke through a hookah, a ceramic flask containing water that cooled the acrid tobacco smoke before it was inhaled.

Two beautiful young women had danced gracefully in the center of the room, seductively swaying to the musicians' high-pitched notes. The dancers' black hair had glistened while falling down to their waists. Each had a shimmering hair clip or band to control the long tresses, as they had moved with the music. Full-length and figure-hugging costumes had covered their shapely figures—one dressed in bright red and the other in dark blue. Their clothes had glittered from the sparkle of pure silver threads woven into the very fabric of the material plus the many colorful sequins edging hems and bodices. Both had been barefooted with a string of bells tied around one ankle.

Adding to the unabashedly suggestive and seductive moves, each woman had worn a knitted string corset tied around her waist, with gleaming bronze medallions hanging from it on silk threads. The metal trinkets swayed and collided with each movement, accentuating the women's undulating hips, in an artful and alluring manner, further capturing the minds and fancies of the men watching.

As the pace of the music had increased, the visually stimulating movements of the beautiful dancers had kept time, the embedded silver strands shimmering, as the medallions bounced and clinked together ever faster. The women's captivating appeal had been inescapable and enchanting, exactly as they had intended.

Azim noted that Tasar had appeared mesmerized watching the dancers and, indeed, his friend had arisen, right after the performance ended. He had asked Azim to join him, but Azim had smiled and waved his second in command away, as his friend had disappeared in search of the two women.

The memories of Maria had returned to him as he had drawn deeply on the hookah in the coffee house. He had bedded other women since his trip to Kostel—where he first fulfilled his manhood—but none had thrilled or stirred him as the young peasant woman in Am Furtt.

A loose stone rolled down the hill and came to rest against his boot, interrupting his reverie on the slope of the Caucasus Mountains. With a shrug, he had one final thought: *When the Derbent campaign is over, I will once again visit the mother of my son.* The prospect of seeing her pleased and warmed him, despite the chill in the air.

Standing and looking around, he called the two goat herders to come forward. Then, he motioned Srdoc to join them. "What is the terrain like from our present location to the single wall?"

The eldest boy gave a cocky grin and answered, "The way is not difficult. We can easily guide you and be there before it is fully dark."

The boy's cousin added, "The wall is one or two ridges north of here, and neither should prove difficult for your camels and troops."

"Thank you, boys. I believe we have no further need for your services. Srdoc, see that these herders are well rewarded and sent on their way. May Allah be with both of you."

"Yes, thank you, Aga and praise be unto thee," the eldest replied, bowing and backing away.

Azim turned and sat down to eat his cold supper. He turned when he heard the sound of a terrifying scream, just as Srdoc lifted the oldest goat herder above his head and hurled him over the edge of the cliff.

The other started to run away, but in his state of terror, he turned right into Tasar's barrel chest. The short man lifted the boy high into the air and he, too, went over the edge, as Azim's second in command shouted, "May the two of you rest in peace, if Allah so grants it. It happens, you know."

Striding up, Srdoc had the evil, crooked smile on his face. He sat down to eat and said, "The young ones are duly rewarded, Aga, and they promised that they will say nothing about our soldiers or where we are headed."

"Very well. We will unload the camels here and distribute the fire pots from the camels to our backpacks. Have fifteen men remain here. They can return down the mountain with the camels at midday tomorrow—but no sooner. Something may delay us, and I do not want to take a chance that the guards on the wall may see them."

"Yes, my Aga."

With the Greek firepots repacked, the soldiers continued climbing the mountain. To Azim, the going was slow, and he began to worry that they might lose the advantage of darkness for their attack the next morning. He and his officers harried the soldiers, urging them on with softly spoken words of encouragement.

Throughout the last of the afternoon and into early evening, they did their best to continue at a fast pace. The ladders and packed Greek fire satchels on their shoulders became galling weights, with straps cutting painfully into their skin, particularly when traveling through gullies and brush-filled depressions. They clawed and overcame the many crests, staying just below hilltops.

At a spiny mountain ridge, they finally reached the single wall that rose starkly above them. Advance scouts saw its dim shape, revealed by the last light of day. They also observed a lighted lantern carried by two sentries walking high up on top of the wall. The advance men brought Azim close so that he could assess the situation. Before he could utter a command, Srdoc was at his side.

"Leave it to me and two of my men, Aga, to get rid of the guards." the tall, husky man said.

Looking at him in the near-darkness, Azim imagined that he saw a glint of excitement in Srdoc's eyes.

"So be it, but be aware that time is against us. We still have many miles to travel, carrying heavy packs. When you have overcome the guards, clap twice and have your troopers continue along the top of the wall. Your men will deal with the next guards and watchtowers in the same fashion as we move toward the main fort. Now hear me clearly—we must not allow any enemy soldier to warn the fort about our presence! Understand?"

Srdoc's reply was a firm grasp of Azim's arm, and then he eased into the dark, like the shadow of a night adder.

"May Allah give you peace and reward you, for your difficulties tonight are dangerous," Azim whispered after him.

The wait seemed endless. He squatted in the darkness, his eyes fixed on the light held by the Persian guards. Then, he lost sight of that light and heard two sharp claps.

"Tasar, see that Srdoc's men begin scaling the wall quickly," he ordered. "Have them attach several ladders end-to-end. I will lead your men until we are all on top and moving toward the fortress." His second set off instantly to carry out his orders.

Only when Azim started up the wall did he appreciate the climbing ability of Srdoc and his men, and the stealth required to scale the fortification and deal with the sentries, all without sounding an alarm. It was a heady climb even using the ladders stacked and affixed three high. Five or six men scaled each set simultaneously, causing the ladders to sway and undulate, forcing climbers to adjust rapidly to maintain their balance.

Azim reached the top and followed Srdoc eastward toward the fort in the moonless night. The troop divided into groups and rigged shielded candle lanterns to light the way for the lead men moving along the top of the wall. Others followed, tied together by a line. A real danger to their operation was that the lights might give away their presence. Undoubtedly, that would trigger a bonfire warning to the fortress. They took every precaution to keep the lamps hooded.

CHAPTER TWENTY-FIVE

Day Three
May 11

Srdoc and his men secured one tower after another with quick dispatch. Most of the Janissary force lagged behind, to minimize the shuffling sounds of the many feet.

Finally, Srdoc's lead men arrived within fifty yards of where the single wall intersected with the main wall of the fortress, which was clearly outlined against the night sky from the glow of lighted torches within the citadel. Cautiously, the Janissaries continued toward the stronghold, only to discover that a large stone guardhouse blocked their final approach. All appeared dark inside, and there were no sounds.

As Azim kneeled beside Srdoc, he asked, "What are your thoughts on this next difficulty?"

"I have already sent one man ahead to scout. Let us wait for his return before we decide on a plan."

"Very well, I will wait beside you." Azim felt the other man bristle at someone looking over his shoulder, but he paid no mind. If the mission failed, his head would be on the chopping block, not that of his lieutenant.

They waited in silence, as Azim passed the word for Tasar to join them. "My friend," he whispered, "a man has been sent ahead to determine what guards are in the block house ahead. Best your troopers begin preparations for the fire bundles that we are going to rain down on the Persians. But forewarn them, no unnecessary noise until the blockhouse is secured."

"So it shall be, my Aga," his second answered.

Azim raised his hand to grasp the man's shoulder. "Peace be with thee, and may the Prophet Mohammed watch over all of us tonight."

"And with thee, my Aga."

Azim waited impatiently until the scout returned.

The man reported, "At least six men are watching or resting behind the walls of the guardhouse, as far as I can tell. The structure has a two-foot-wide ledge on either side, and the walls are waist-high. Above, there is a hexagonal roof and six side openings, each facing in different directions."

"Good work," Azim commented. Turning to Srdoc, he asked, "Well, what is it to be? How do we take it without alerting the main fort?"

"I will have ten of my men crawl silently and swiftly to the guardhouse and kill all the Persian soldiers."

Azim deliberated, then asked with a touch of impatience, "And how, exactly, will they do that—silently? Perhaps one will stand up and ask the way to the nearest brothel?" he chided, derisively. "Or, maybe, you have a magic ointment that will make us invisible to the enemy, so that our men may slit the Persian throats at their leisure." He could not see his second's face, but he felt the man's animosity at his bitter sarcasm.

Finally, Srdoc said, "We will create a diversion."

"That is exactly my thought!"

Srdoc ordered his men forward. Two scaled down the wall, with orders to make their way stealthily about twenty yards to one side of the imposing structure. Perhaps they did; no one knew, as they immediately disappeared into the moonless darkness. The other dozen men crawled quietly along the top of the wall toward the guards.

"How will those men attacking the blockhouse know when the men on the ground are ready?" Azim asked in a whispered voice.

"Simple, my Aga, one of my men below, who speaks Persian, will call out to the guards asking for help."

"Excellent," he replied.

They waited impatiently. Time passed slowly, and Azim had to use all of his self-control to give the appearance of calmness. The entire operation now hinged on silently neutralizing the defenders. Finally, he asked, "What is your second plan if the first fails?"

"It will not, as I have sent my best men. If they encounter something unexpected and are overwhelmed, I will order the rest of my men to charge immediately. It will be costly, but my troops *will* kill the guards."

"What about the sounds of fighting?"

"That can be a problem. In that event, it is important that all of us be ready to rush forward to breach the fortress wall."

"Let us hope that it will not come to that, and that Allah watches over us this morning."

More minutes passed without any sound or sign of activity. Azim was on the verge of ordering the charge, when they heard rocks tumbling down the sharp hillside to the right of the wall, followed by a panicked voice shouting in Persian, "Help me, someone in the guardhouse, please help me! I have fallen off the path in the dark and broken my leg."

Azim and his men would never know how convincing the cry was to capture the attention of the guards, because, at the same instant the distraction occurred, Srdoc's men rose as one, springing their surprise attack and fell on the guards and their strategic position.

A lighted hooded lantern swung from the blockhouse. It was the signal for the balance of Srdoc's men to run toward the main fortress wall, and indeed, Azim and his entire force.

Azim ran to where the single wall intersected with the main fort.

Srdoc was already there, kneeling and gazing down toward the gate area. He turned as Azim knelt beside him. "No one appears to have been alerted by our taking the blockhouse.

"Allah be praised!"

"The arch opening for the gate is not visible from here, Aga. I propose to keep my men on the parapet walkway and make our way toward that far corner, above the gate," he said pointing. "At some point, we should have a clear drop down on ropes to the main level, where we can overtake the sentries. Once secure, I will send my best archers to the tower. They will shoot all who try to stop us from opening the gate. In the meantime, we will have to hold off any troops who might come down the lanes, until Tasar's men have completed their assignment with the fire pots."

"Good. As soon as we have control of the Mountain Wall Gate, designate two bowmen to shoot flaming signal arrows aimed at our army outside the walls. That will be the sign for our multitude of archers to let loose their burning arrows and for our horsemen to toss lighted torches over the wall. Tell them to shoot as many signals as needed, until the night sky fills with incoming arrows, which will let us know that they have received our message. At the same time, all the brothers of our Janissary division will move toward the gate. Make certain all the lanes in the citadel are covered by your archers so that our troops are not surprised by an attack from the rear, just as we planned."

"It shall be so, Aga."

"Good fortune to thee and may the true Prophet keep you and your men safe."

In the flickering dim light of lit torches inside the citadel, Azim watched some of Srdoc's men rappel down ropes while their leader and the remainder of the men hurried along the battlement. *That man knows how to lead soldiers,* he concluded. *Scaling the wall and successfully dealing with the sentries at the watchtowers were impressive feats.*

In the next instant, loud shouts and the clanging noises of men, fighting with swords, interrupted his thoughts. Unforeseen, there was an early morning change of the Persian guards at the gate, doubling the number. Quickly, Srdoc and more of his men rappelled down from the parapet walkway to help overcome the defenders. That left fewer men guarding against counter-attacks along the high walkways above the gate area.

At the same time, Tasar's men quickly spread out along the battlement, which allowed them to position themselves nearly around the entire periphery of the *Naryn-Kala* portion of the citadel. The barrel-chested man raised his arm high, ready to give the signal to sling the Greek firepots, as he expectantly watched for Azim's command. At the ready, his troops held shielded candles burning to light the fuses.

Turning toward Tasar, who was standing on the wall to his left, Azim cupped his hands and shouted, *"WE ARE IN IT NOW! LET LOOSE THE FIRE POTS!"*

Tasar dropped his arm, and some three hundred urns flew in the first flight, sending thin trails of light arching high overhead, faintly visible against the black morning sky. The flaming pots burst upon impact, and the black ooze ignited everything it touched, even adhering to stone walls and columns. At first, the fires remained confined to the places of initial impact. As more pottery crashed down, the blaze jumped dramatically, like a leaf caught up in the wind, rolling along, as though the fires themselves were in control—moving along rooftops, courtyard rafters and pathways throughout the *Naryn-Kala*—with the oily substance even spreading atop bathhouse pools and fountains. The sharp stench of the blazing thick ooze was overpowering, as a huge dark cloud of smoke rose into the air.

At first, there was a sleepy chorus of shouted alarms to greet the danger, as people awoke and soldiers began to fill the square. A chaotic scene followed as Persians ran into each other, exiting out of their houses, trying to avoid the falling oil bombs while assessing the situation. Azim heard contradictory orders issued in Persian, as military officers sought to cope with the attack while each was mindful of his own safety from the falling crockery.

What the *Naryn-Kala* experienced was only the beginning. Moments after the clay urns began falling, the flaming signal arrow took flight toward the Turkish lines. Immediately, everyone became aware of a new peril, as hundreds—no thousands—of blazing arrows arched into the heavens, became distant pinpoints of light high above in the dark sky and then dropped with deadly intent throughout the city. Flight after flight fell, as an unending and uninterrupted sea of burning killer arrows poured down on Derbent from above, each shaft wrapped with a patch of blazing pitch-soaked linen cloth.

Adding to the light show in the predawn darkness, red-hot shot from artillery cannons streaked brightly through the sky in a continuous display of blazing fireballs. Even more terrorizing were the projectiles launched by the five catapults, the large, gangly torsion-operated hurling machines, which sent flaming balls of pitch high over the tall walls to smash structures inside the fortified city, engulfing everything in flames. As though that was not enough, the monster Ottoman siege gun roared from two miles away, and its horrific shock wave froze the furious action of both defenders and invaders for a split instant throughout the fortress and battlefield area.

As thousands of burning missiles continued to fall from the sky, predawn darkness became unnaturally bright, in part from the continuing fire bombardments, and partially from clouds of burnt powder and smoke that drifted overhead, which mirrored a city in flames.

CHAPTER TWENTY-SIX

As Azim dropped down a rope to the battlement walkway, he drew his *yatagan* and rushed toward the corner of the fort, where Persian soldiers were streaming toward the Mountain Wall Gate area.

Almost at once, he found himself confronting two Persian guards, each carrying a pike, a long wooden pole with an integrated metal spear and hook at one end.

They charged as he scrambled backward, deflecting the thrust of the first spear with his sword. The rapid forward motion of the two attackers carried them slightly past Azim's defensive position, as he ducked behind a stone column located along the battlement, which permitted him to thrust his sword into the back of one soldier. The defender dropped his pike, slipped and fell to the pavement below near the gate. The other man quickly wheeled about and charged at him again.

Instantly kneeling beside the stone column, Azim twisted his sword upward into the man's midsection, severing his spine. The Persian soldier rigidly gripped his pike, but his momentum took him over the edge, still impaled by Azim's sword.

The top of all arched gates carried the same name, "the murder hole," because all such openings allowed defenders to drop stones or burning oil on attackers attempting to breach the perimeter through the gateway. Unprepared for Azim's troops and the surprise attack, the hole was unmanned at that moment of the morning. Azim picked up the dead Persian soldier's pike and became the defender of his men below that treacherous opening. Several Persian soldiers ran toward him, as he swung the lance in a complete roundabout circle, knocking one defender over the side of the exterior wall.

With the man's anguished howl of terror and death ringing in his ears, Azim reflected for an instant, on how useful the pike was as a weapon. He had not used one since he was a young soldier.

The other Persian barreled toward him, a big man with broad shoulders, and brought his sword down heavily on the staff of the pike, splitting the wood and lopping off several feet of the pole. The sword's downward arc smashed against the stone walkway and broke the sword's blade off at the handle.

The soldier stood up, hurled the hilt away and drew a long, curved knife from his waist belt. Blinking rapidly to counter sweat running into his eyes, the large man confronted Azim from a crouched position, his blade weaving from side to side.

Azim also drew his knife, and the two fighters warily circled each other.

"Now, you Ottoman devil," the Persian screamed, "you will squeal like a pig in the throes of death when my knife splits your belly wide open. Will you beg for mercy, you Turkish son of a whore, or do you have enough nerve to continue fighting me, man to man?"

Azim did not understand all the soldier's words, but he comprehended enough and smiled, thinly.

In a move of supreme cockiness, the soldier casually tossed his knife from one hand to the other, feinted with a left jab, then just as coolly returned the curved blade to his right hand. The Persian thrust it low, aiming for Azim's thigh, in an attempt to cripple him. Instead, the sharp blade sliced through Azim's clothing and pricked his skin in a long, superficial cut.

Rapidly, Azim gave ground, to avoid the silver blade again, and he took refuge behind the stone column.

The soldier stared at him and laughed. Apparently feeling supremely confident with his skills as a knife fighter, the big man lunged again—then again.

Nimbly, Azim darted from side to side, keeping the column between them.

The Persian continued the furious attack, slashing one way, then another, while loudly shrieking at Azim. There was no mistaking one obvious fact—that man intended to kill him.

Dodging and ducking behind the stone column, Azim waited patiently for his chance. Then, the soldier lunged once more, and Azim countered, intending to stab the assailant in the arm. Instead, his knife tangled in the soldier's chain mail and, inexplicably, it spun out of Azim's sweaty fingers. Suddenly, his situation was desperate.

Feverish and beside himself at the favorable turn of events, the enemy soldier charged at Azim, his knife held high, aimed at Azim's chest to finish the fight.

At the last moment, Azim managed to step to the side and beneath the flashing blade. Seeing the end of the wooden pike lying on the walkway, he quickly grabbed it. Once more, the defender charged, again with his knife held high, but Azim, wielding the pole ruthlessly, struck the man across the side of the head, sending the soldier's helmet flying over the wall.

Dazed by the blow, the warrior reeled unsteadily.

Quickly, Azim was on him from behind, pressing the shaft of the pike against the man's throat.

Instinctively, the Persian dropped to his knees, and the momentum flung Azim over the soldier's back and onto the solid stone walkway.

Both men arose at the same instant, each gripping the arm of the other, and circled in a death spiral.

Without warning, Azim snapped his head forward and solidly struck the big man on the bridge of his nose. As blood gushed from the dazed soldier's nose, Azim stepped closer and kneed the man hard in the crotch, catching him squarely and crushing his genitals. Holding the Persian from behind, Azim frog-marched the screaming man to an opening at the edge of the wall and pushed him over the side.

The enemy soldier's shriek was horrifyingly loud and ended when the man struck the ground thirty feet below.

Wheezing heavily, Azim managed to mumble, "Farewell to a worthy opponent, indeed, but not commendable enough on this day." For a moment, he slumped against the outer wall, exhausted from the hand-to-hand fighting. In the *Naryn-Kala*, the flames started by Greek firebombs served their purpose of distracting attention away from the Mountain Wall Gate, while producing an overpowering stench and rolling, thick black clouds of smoke.

From the booming sounds emanating at the other end of the fortress, Azim imagined the carnage that was taking place, as one cannonade after another hammered the Derbent fortress walls near the sea. The bombardment was nonstop, and he expected that the city at the other end of the fort was fully ablaze.

Then, suddenly and with no forewarning, a comparative stillness overtook the entire battlefield, as Turkish artillery pieces and catapults ceased firing while reverberations slowly dissipated and became increasingly distant echoes. The strange quiet was not absolute. Anyone standing on the southern battlement walkways, like Azim, heard the noises of soldiers, equipment and animals moving about. Still, the muted calm to the prior violent crashes of cannons and catapults were welcomed by defenders hunkered down inside the walls. Some knew what came next; others became unnerved, and a few prayed that maybe—just maybe—the Turks had withdrawn. The hopes of the latter were purely naive.

As the relative calm continued, Azim pushed himself up, looked both ways along the parapet and saw no defenders approaching. The top of the murder hole was secure for the moment, as he looked down to the area below, where blood made footing treacherously slippery for everyone.

Srdoc and his men were trying to work loose the massive wooden crossbeam that locked the heavy gate like a lever. Usually, defenders inside the fort moved the beam up or down with the assistance of a heavy counterweight. A drum with spokes allowed several men to turn the mechanism, winding or unwinding the thick hemp cable that ran through several pulleys located high up on the structure and then out to the end of the heavy crossbeam. A Persian soldier had cut the cable earlier, leaving it dangling several feet away from stone steps that led from the gate area up to the murder hole and battlement walkway where Azim stood.

Other enemy defenders now were coming toward Azim along the wall's walkway. He slashed his way toward them, using only the head of the pike, when Tasar suddenly appeared at his side, hacking and plunging his razor-sharp sword through Persian troops with wild abandonment. On a roof above the passageway, Azim saw an enemy archer stretching his bow, and instinctively, he drew a pistol from Tasar's waistband, cocked it and fired. The archer dropped into the milling and fighting throng below. Azim returned to look down the murder hole again. The gate must be unlocked immediately.

Srdoc and his men were attempting to raise the heavy oak beam, using their shoulders and backs. However, there was little movement, despite the strain of their bulging muscles.

Seeing the issue, Azim shouted, "Srdoc, have as many of your troops as possible hang onto that counterweight rope, and let us see if their combined weight will help lift the beam while you and your men continue to heave upwards from below."

The tall man looked up at him and nodded. The light from the many fires burning out of control in this part of the fort momentarily reflected off his sweat-covered body and evil offset smile. Additionally, the first light of false dawn was on the horizon, better lighting the battle scene at the gate.

One Janissary soldier heard the order and jumped from the steps, hanging onto the hemp cable. A second attempted to grasp the legs of the first man, but failed and fell to his death on the blood-washed stones below. Soon, though, another grabbed onto the cable, then a third, and so on. Those straining to lift the beam on the ground found that it was moving. Between the two efforts, the substantial wooden crossbar rose slowly, until it was standing upright, and men tied off the line to hold it in an open position.

Oddly, and almost on cue, it was at that moment that the Ottoman musicians began playing their discordant notes, with kettledrums steadily booming, fifes whistling and horns trumpeting. The sounds proved to be a brief precursor for what came next.

An earth-trembling roar arose and rolled through the air, permeating everything and reverberating off nearby hills, as more than forty-five thousand Turkish troops rushed the broken walls near the Caspian Sea, brandishing their swords, spears, pikes and shields—yelling as loud as they could. For the Persian defenders, it must have sounded as though the world was ending, as fear gripped the city and its people. The magnificent defensive walls no longer could withstand the onslaught of modern Ottoman firepower and the Turkish Army.

At the same time, Srdoc and his men muscled and swung open the massive, metal-clad Mountain Wall Gate. Immediately, the Janissary division on the other side poured through—a surge of screaming Turks adding to the unbelievably loud cacophony of noise, all rushing downhill to entrap the Persian defenders. They were an unstoppable military force that included Azim and his troops—a wave of warriors snaking through narrow passageways, lanes and portals—wildly slashing and overrunning defenders.

Aga Abdul Azim found a discarded sword and brandished it, while participating in the thousands of individual skirmishes, as the Janissaries rapidly moved downhill toward the Caspian Sea, buttressed by the advantage of surprise and momentum. His weapon ran with blood as he and others finally reached the defensive line of Persian soldiers at the eastern end of the fort's shattered walls. Confronted with two merging and simultaneous attacks, the Persians turned and fled through the citadel's gates on the other side of the fort—allowing a vast number of city residents and Persian soldiers to escape. Imam Kulu also fled the field, leaving half of his army dead upon the battlefield. By noon, the fight for Derbent was over.

Despite the seemingly invincible defensive might and power of one of the most heavily fortified cities in the known world, Azim knew it was a great victory for Ottoman forces, as the entire region swiftly fell on that third day. Yet, the Turkish attack had begun badly on the first day as the Ottomans tried unsuccessfully to draw Persian horsemen away from the fortress walls and into an ambush of waiting cannon fire. The plan failed, and few Persians died from the deception while the Turks suffered over one thousand casualties.

On the second day, Turkish cannon bombardments significantly broke through the fortifications located nearest to the Caspian Sea, laying waste to the walls.

As Azim reviewed the events of the last three days, it was evident that the Persian commanders expected the Ottoman attack on the third day to take place at the site of the ruined walls, as a simple matter of logic, and so it was. The unexpected event was the flanking attack by the main body of Janissary warriors from the mountain end of the fort, as they executed a classic military pincer movement. In total, Persian prisoners exceeded no more than three thousand out of a force that began the fight at sixty thousand.

Forever after, the three-day battle became known as the *Battle of Torches*, given the action that occurred in the brightly lit darkness of the third morning.

High praise and recognition went to Aga Abdul Azim and his men, for their heroism and successful surprise attack. Honoring outstanding bravery was customary in the Ottoman Army. As rewards, the commanding pashas gave Azim's troops first choice to select their share from the city's spoils, including Derbent women.

For Azim, he chose a chest of gold coins and a dark-eyed beauty. He returned with his treasures to an opulent, vacant dwelling in the *Naryn-Kala* area, which was untouched by the firebombing. Taken by the woman's graceful figure and haunting eyes, Azim tried to recapture the heat of his first encounter years earlier in Am Furtt. The woman left him unfulfilled. He yearned for only one—the lowly serf living in Kostel with flashing blue eyes named Maria.

Afterward, he dismissed the woman and rested by himself. As happened with increasing frequency, he found his thoughts wandering, recalling the small farming hamlet, Maria—the serf—and thinking about his son. With the end of the five-year period approaching since he was last in Kostel, he began to count down the time for his next visit to the Kupa River Valley.

Book III
Helena's War
Fiefdom of Kostel

CHAPTER TWENTY-SEVEN

Saint George's Day
Market Kostel
1694

The gusle stopped, and the crowd moved about, stretching to loosen stiff joints and muscles. Johannes Stefanich drank from his flask once more, then resumed plucking the strings on his instrument. He remained silent, as the rake of his blue eyes took in the gathering, and rested briefly on the nobles seated on their cushioned chairs.

During his narration, he observed the eyes of more than one serf straying to watch Baron Johann Michele Androcha, a man in his thirties, and Count Lamberg, when he described the argument between Helena and the former Lord of Kostel.

As Johannes traveled the river valley and beyond, his discussions with men at all levels revealed the increasing tensions between the nobility, who demanded and collected taxes for themselves as well as the Emperor, and the hard working serfs who spent their lives providing it. One consequence was that the serf population, over countless decades, remained relatively unchanged due to high rates of mortality, particularly among children, resulting from the limitations of food and goods available to sustain families. He had heard one example to illustrate their plight when he had attended the University. A study found that many serf families could set aside only enough extra wool to provide a single new winter coat for each family member about every decade.

He had heard rumors that new crops were making their way across Europe, which originated in distant lands across the oceans—such as a heartier strain of hemp, new grains called maize and a distinctively new fruit called tomatoes. These might improve the lives of serfs, but it would take years before they arrived in Kostel and, ultimately be planted, grown and, inevitably, taxed.

He had smiled inwardly, as he noticed the parish bishop squirming in his high-back chair when he described how Helena had accused Bishop Juris of hiding behind solid walls of rock. In the story, he knew that the priest's explanation of remaining in the castle at the time of the attack sounded logical, but trite and hollow, despite the spiritual sway of the clergy in the fiefdom and the love people bestowed on their local Catholic men of piety.

Johannes briefly considered the clergy's paradoxical position on taxes. The Church received one-third of all taxes levied on serfs; it was its primary source of income. This left the religious order walking a thin line, and sometimes one that was nearly invisible, between tending to the souls of their parishioners, and facilitating and perpetuating tax levies on the same flock. Additionally, it was useful for the clergy to have a productive and harmonious relationship with the nobility, even though leaseholders changed from time to time. After all, it was the Castle Lord and his men who set tax rates and enforced the collection, including the church's share.

Lastly, news of changes had already come to his ears, as Vienna experimented with ways to increase revenue, lower costs and administer its vast land holdings differently. Efforts were already underway in some areas of the kingdom to reduce fief overhead, by appointing only a captain of the guard, whose duties included both administrative and enforcement functions, thereby reducing the cost of one major fiefdom position—that of the expensive and lavish castle lord.

"My friends," the storyteller resumed, as he commanded the attention of the crowd, once more:

> I heard long ago
> And in this way
> So the truth I say
> For all to know

"Serfs died in Kostel, as a result of the Turkish attack, during the winter in the year of our Lord, fifteen hundred and eighty through the following year. The gap in family continuity created by missing and dying children lasted for years. Even today, after five generations, evidence of the lost children remains. And, the ill will between serfs and the fiefdom lord simmered." As he spoke, he looked at the nobility seated on their down-filled cushions and noted a ripple of uneasy movement, as men crossed their legs and women shifted in the chairs.

"Time appeared suspended, yet the five years since the previous Turkish raid flew by, as the people of Am Furtt lived, farmed, survived, planned and built defenses against the next assault. Through all the madness and preparation, the village matriarch, Helena, in her bright clothes, was a pillar of strength that drove the war committee of village elders and then the villagers themselves.

"Repairs and rebuilding the drying sheds took years, between all the daily and heavy seasonal farming chores. Some of you in the audience may not be familiar with life on a hide." He tried very hard not to look at Baron Androcha when he made the comment. He was not successful.

"Eventually, the village committee began to gather itself, and ideas were suggested, discussed, and either dismissed or retained for future consideration. Helena kept the process going, requiring the men to focus on matters where they had little or no experience. They abandoned the previous strategy of hiding in the cave, and laid out ideas for a series of physical barriers, intending to slow any hard-charging enemy on horseback, thereby permitting a more organized defense against swiftly moving attackers.

"Furthermore, they had to guess and plan on the route the Turks would use to arrive at their village. It was certain that the marauders had to traverse the Kupa River with their heavy carts. That meant that they could come from the south and cross at Am Furtt using the toll barge, or they might arrive over the road bordering the river from the west. This would require them to cross the river many miles farther up the mountains. Aga Azim's words of surprise, and of remaining undetected before his next arrival, rang in Helena's mind. They eliminated from consideration the road from Gottschee to the north because the castle's long-range cannons covered that approach.

"From the hillside forests, the villagers logged a significant number of trees to build their defenses. They buried many on end, to create walls at the toll crossing shaped in the form of a funnel leading to and from the river. It was wide enough only for a horse or an ox-drawn cart to pass. Further, the posts forming the walls were too tall for a horse to jump, yet spacing between allowed villagers to thrust a spear or to shoot an arrow. As the mouth of the funnel widened, the villagers added thorn bushes, painfully transplanted from the forest, to lengthen the barrier along the edges of their fields.

"Slowly, those and other ideas were implemented in the time remaining..."

CHAPTER TWENTY-EIGHT

Am Furtt
1583-84

"Antonio," Helena asked, "you are an excellent hunter and always bring down an elk to add to your stock of winter food. I have a question for you. Is it possible to light a pile of logs with a burning arrow?" She pointed to a stack of cut wood.

"Yes, I think so, although I have never tried it," the man paused, then answered. "You need dry straw and kindling to ignite it, just like a fireplace. And it would be well to douse the wood with the distilled spirits from fir trees so that it catches fire quickly."

"Can you teach other bowmen to do the same?" she asked."

"Of course, with practice," the man said.

Helena continued, "I have in mind asking the castle lord to station three or four bowmen to assist us when the time comes. Further, I would like you to train six or seven men from our village in archery. That will give us the flexibility to use them in various ways. Will you do that, Antonio?"

"Yes, of course."

Steffan saw to the placement of wood posts as barriers, in a checkered pattern, along and around paths in the village. It allowed wagons to circle the obstacle, but hard-charging Turks on horseback would have to slow. Nearby, disguised blinds provided hiding places for archers.

Helena recalled the descriptions the Turkish aga shared with Maria. Of particular interest was the number of Bosnian brigands that were part of his troop. That gave her another idea—playing on the mystical superstition and fears of those men. Working alone, she drew the outline of an evil symbol in the dirt with a stick, making sure to include hex signs taken from the commonly held beliefs and legends of yore—particularly the Bosnians. The result was a hexagon with spokes, displaying both the Christian symbols for Jesus' crucifixion and Saint Petar's murder while nailed upside-down to a cross. Her idea was to paint and show such evil-eye designs upon the sides of drying sheds and on wooden signs mounted in various locations around and throughout the village. She tried to persuade Steffan to begin painting and constructing the mystical signs.

"Nana," he asked, "what in heaven's name will such hex signs do for us? How in the hell will it deter hard-charging Muslims from hacking off our heads with their flashing swords?"

"Ah, my son, do not use terms of blasphemy. Think of my dearly departed husband making his way through purgatory."

"I am sorry. I know how much you miss him, as all of us do. He was your strength, as he was mine, too."

"Believe me, flesh of my flesh, when we add a bleached skull from our back yard to each sign, it will cause the spirit-believers to quiver. It may be ineffective against the Turkish soldiers, but I believe it will unnerve the others, seeing the skulls' empty eye sockets and grinning teeth, and it will remind them of their fears about ghosts and the dark unknown depths beyond death."

"I pray it will," Steffan replied, but the skepticism on his face was obvious to her. "I cannot help with your idea. For all I know, *Stari's* remains may be among the group. The thought is too gruesome for me! If you insist on going ahead with this, please ask someone else to perform the task."

"As you wish," she said, scowling. "Their belief in the supernatural is an advantage for us. Our job is to have them dwell on their Illyrian myths, turning their minds from us to the black arts. Any panic we can create among the Bosnian irregulars allows us to stampede them more easily toward the castle and its large cannons. I think it is worth trying." Still, another villager undertook the task.

A dozen pagan signs were drawn and attached to log barriers and trees around the village. Painted ones appeared on the sides of storage sheds and barns. In fact, the approach to Am Furtt became unmistakable with the repeated sorcerer icons. At Helena's firm insistence, skulls adorned the center of each, with an arrow extending through the gaping cavities. They were ugly reminders of the previous raid, and it stiffened the resolve of most villagers.

Still, some passing travelers along the busy ferry road objected to the grisly hex signs, believing them blasphemous, and they petitioned the Bishop of Fara to visit the village and opine.

Dressed in his white caftan and adorned with his gilded cross hanging around his neck, the Catholic leader in Kostel arrived riding a donkey, along with a retinue of two priests, attired in brown woolen tunics.

Bishop Juris commented, "I believe I understand what you are attempting, Helena," after viewing the symbols and listening to her explanation. The man looked perplexed, and he shook his head several times during Helena's description, particularly when she spoke of adding skulls. At one point, he seemed dismayed and was about to speak.

Quickly, Helena instructed Maria, "Please serve our most honored guest, dear, with the best wine in the house, and also bring out the jug of *rakia,* as he may prefer that. And here, honored Bishop, please help yourself to these fresh slices of *potica.*"

"Ah," the bishop sighed, ravishing a slice of rolled bread filled with honey-soaked walnuts. Maria filled his glass with the stronger of the two drinks. "Nothing as gratifying as a delicacy, and I am particularly partial to this rolled sweet bread." With his mouth nearly full, he washed the delightful treat down with another glass of the strong, clear liquor.

As soon as the bishop's glass emptied, either Maria or Helena refilled it.

Seeing the increasingly languid state of the churchman, Helena pressed her point. "Dear Bishop, we need every advantage possible against the brutality of the Turks and their warlike ways. They refuse to believe in heaven, so playing on their fears of the dead is one way to try to unnerve the heathens. Please permit us to use this trick, along with the other things we have planned. We pray for strength from God, and we know you will ask Him to help when the raiders return. You already know that Am Furtt villagers are God-fearing souls and have great love and respect for you and the Church. I assure you that we have not changed in that regard."

The bishop's mood appeared to mellow after consuming several more glasses of *rakia* and another three pieces of freshly baked *potica*. "Blessed be thee, Helena, and thee, Maria," he said, and sprinkled holy water on them, which appeared magically at his side, supplied by one of his companions. He then made his way to the village's small Virgin Mary Sanctuary and bowed in prayer for all who might be injured or killed in *Helena's War*, as most Kostelians called the anticipated conflict. Turning to the two women, he added, "I will inform the congregation of my blessing at Sunday Mass. The lords in both castles, Brod and Kostel, will wish for no interruption of trade across the Kupa. While the heathen symbols are unusual, they are proper, due to the imminent threat from the Turkish barbarians. My blessing will sanctify this part of your plan, Helena."

"Holy Father, thank you for your understanding," Maria said, falling to her knees in gratitude before him and kissing the ring on his extended finger.

"And, Helena," the priest continued, "I will personally sing out ten verses upon my return to Fara, to speed Petar's travel through purgatory. I believe his journey nears its end."

Helena cried out with joy, and both women bowed their heads respectfully, as the holy man mounted his donkey and rode away, clutching several slices of the sweet bread in his hand. The Bishop of Fara's news about Petar energized the family, and indeed, everyone in the village, to tackle the other planned defensive projects.

———◆———◆———

Over the intervening years, the villagers rebuilt two drying sheds burned by the Turks, except the one of

Rado's conception. Steffan and other villagers spent many months thinking about a new design for that structure. Additionally, Steffan was in the midst of designing a powerful new weapon for the inside of the structure.

Steffan told the men working on this project, "We will rebuild this shed, and it will contain a new killing machine that we will call the 'spiked fist of God.' Perhaps we will build two 'fists,' one for each hand. But these must deliver a deadly force, sufficient to kill any enemy or horseman in its path."

One villager described them as weapons that would "smite their enemies to eternal damnation."

The building began to take shape with the plan drawn and finalized on a flat board using a blackened charcoal stick. The structure was much taller and wider than the previous one, which required stouter support timbers. Trees with trunks nearly two feet in diameter would become upright posts, and their number doubled on each side, compared to the original shed. Further, the structure would need to be solidly cross-braced and reinforced to handle the stresses of the large weapons that Steffan had in mind.

The heavy work involved all the men from the village and volunteers from other hamlets. Serfs used the tools that were available—braces, pulleys, wedges, heavily braided hemp cables, shovels, picks and teams of oxen—as well as their brute strength.

Some men expressed skepticism on their ability to place the much larger upright posts into the foundation holes. Steffan considered the problem and arrived at a solution. "We will elevate a tree trunk at one end with wedges to create an incline, then pack dirt beneath for temporary support. We will repeat this over and over until each massive log slides into its three-foot-deep foundation hole. Then, we will start on the next post."

When the support posts were in place, they constructed the heavily cross-beamed ceiling and roof. Steffan knew the structure would undergo its greatest strains here. "I hope that my post and beam design is sturdy enough to disperse the stresses to the ground by way of the perimeter uprights."

It took them three years to complete all the projects with Steffan driving the men. It was a massive undertaking for the limited resources available to the hamlet. The Castle Lord refused to allow his soldiers to participate, claiming they had other important duties to perform. When hearing this news, Helena shrugged her shoulders, knowing that another day was coming.

With the shed completed, the men logged and dragged the two heavy tree trunks needed for constructing the twin fists of God. Steffan was everywhere—working, giving directions and providing encouragement.

"We begin with a single log," he explained, "two feet in diameter and ten feet in length. Upright, it is long enough to reach from the shed's rafters to within two feet of the dirt floor. A hole in the log at the top will fasten each to stout ceiling timbers with a linchpin, allowing the weapon to swing freely in a full arc while staying within the confines of the shed."

Affixing the first log took much effort and the aid of three teams of oxen. Then, Steffan gave his next instructions. "Now we will fasten two smaller logs horizontally on the main trunk, as crosspieces," he instructed. "These will strike either a man on foot or a horse and rider, as the weapon moves through its arc and is closest to the ground."

Upon completion, the men drilled ten holes along the leading edge in every crosspiece and then drove metal blades through with heavy hammers. Over a period of many weeks, they filed and sharpened the three-foot-long metal pieces into lethal stilettos.

"Our last task on this fist," he informed those working with him, "is to place this large granite boulder behind the T-junction and attach it in place with a web of thick leather strapping. I figure that the combined falling weight and momentum of the tree trunk and stone are sufficient to impale any man wearing armor or a mounted soldier when the fist moves through its sweep inside the shed."

The completed weapons appeared ungainly—but also ingenious. From its pendulum-like fastening high in the rafters, they would be stored in the darkened area of the raised ceiling. While not hidden, they also would not be obvious. Additionally, their swings differed. One arced from the shed's sidewalls while the other moved from end to end. Simple levers, mounted on the walls, triggered the individual release of each weapon.

It was important to Steffan that they test each weapon, although the thought also made him nervous, thinking about the strain on the building. Despite his reservations, the villagers tested each. The enormous stresses on upright posts, beams and braces during the trials were quite evident. Swinging structural parts screeched and squealed with ear-splitting volume, while dense blue smoke, generated by fire-hot wood chafing against wood, streamed from the thickly greased linchpins. For an instant, the entire structure almost seemed to raise off its embedded moorings, as the weapon swung through the arc of its semicircle. To the villagers and Steffan's delight, everything held together as planned. Then, the serfs and oxen strained to pull the fists up to the ceiling for storage.

Helena instructed Steffan to pain a huge hex sign on top of the newest shed, in the same format as the others, except larger, so that it was visible from every direction. "And also paint another sign," she added, "that says, 'RADO IS HERE.' The Turkish commander should know where to find his son, and you must bait the trap to draw him in to meet the weapons you designed." With a quirky smile, she went on. "Besides, we do not want those Turkish and Bosnian vermin in our farmhouses, looking under our quilts and beds."

Steffen laughed. "All right, Nana, just as you request, but no skull on this one," he insisted.

"Of course not! It could not be seen from any great distance."

CHAPTER TWENTY-NINE

Besides the massive weapons in the shed, Steffan wanted a personal weapon that he could use in hand-to-hand fighting against the brigands—one where his farming skills might give him an advantage. He spent many hours talking and planning with Vincentius Basich, the blacksmith in Fara. They settled on developing a weapon they called a war scythe.

Every farm had a scythe as a cutting tool—it was a workhorse tool—mowing and harvesting hay and grasses. With its long, curved blade, the device might be adapted as a weapon. Certainly, the number of farming accidents involving the tool over the years could attest to its lethal capabilities.

Swinging the implement was rhythmic, within a cutting sweep limited by the length of the wooden handle and, of course, a man's arm, leg and back strength. Usually, a man coiled his body to the right, gripping two handholds attached to the wooden shaft, and swung the sharp curved edge of the blade to the left, just above ground level, leaving cuttings behind. As a weapon, its advantages included extended reach and striking power.

Wielding the blade to the left, then recoiling again for the next cut, required considerable, sustained effort. As a weapon, it locked the cutter into right and left body motions, making the man vulnerable to spear or sword thrusts between regular swings of the implement. Steffan's upper-body strength was legendary, resulting from his years of working the fields and using a scythe. What he needed was a more agile tool of war that he could use to counter slashing and sharp Turkish *yatagans* or pikes.

With the help of Vincentius, the two men considered many improvements to the familiar farm tool, and they tried several different designs. First, Vincentius thickened and hardened the blade and shortened it to thirty inches, reducing the weight. Then, he drew the metal out, pounding it with a heavy hammer against his anvil, thinning it to a fine cutting edge. Using a whetstone, he sharpened the blade to a fine edge. Repeatedly, they soaked and dried the oak handle until it became nearly as strong as bronze, yet lighter. For better control, they added soft leather coverings to the two grips. Although this version weighed less and, therefore, it was agiler, it still required Steffen to cock his body to the right and swing the blade through to the left, leaving intact the same original problem.

After many months of trial and error, the two men hit upon using a shorter oak shaft that held two blades, one at each end facing in opposite directions. After more trials, Vincentius forged new blades, each shaped with a greater curve. With this arrangement, Steffen was able to attack around the edge of an enemy shield, if required. Additionally, each blade was mounted and offset at the end of the handle, leaving ten inches of metal protruding beyond the shaft, similar to the smaller but sharp end of

a pike. The changes permitted Steffan to sweep the legs of an opponent, or use the short segment for stabbing. With the two-blade design, the most important advantage was that it eliminated the need for Steffan to "coil" his body in the traditional manner.

"This weapon looks fearsome," Steffan observed. "But, I still feel it is too heavy."

"I can do something about that," the blacksmith responded. Over time, he drilled holes in each metal blade, to reduce overall weight while retaining the blades' killing integrity. It was exactly what the weapon required.

"The stock may be too brittle," Steffan noted. "It has to be stouter, or a strong sword will take it down."

"Ah, you will get used to it," the blacksmith insisted. "We will soak each end in water to swell the joints holding the blades. Then, I will add iron pins to fasten each blade securely to the oak handle. It will feel like everything is one piece. Think of it as the peasant's weapon, delivered directly from the Lord, Himself—a proper war scythe for a serf experienced in farming! Then, Steffan, I think you should paint it black. That will make it look even more menacing to an adversary."

"Good idea! I will use it to kill the murdering bastards," Steffan growled.

Painted black, it, indeed, looked evil, and the curved iron blades appeared wicked. Steffan held the staff in the middle, his hands spread wide along the shaft. He practiced until it became a lethal force when worked in a continuous back and forth motion. With each of Vincentius' modifications, the dual-bladed scythe became evermore a weapon for slaughtering his enemies. At least, Steffan hoped it would be, and that he would not be the one bleeding on the ground, or decapitated by his opponent.

He practiced cutting one straw "enemy" after another until he perfected his motions and knew it would be effective in close quarters. As his muscles strengthened, he wielded the weapon with greater nimbleness and authority.

Then, Vincentius had still another idea. He drilled a hole in the middle of the oak shaft, with his hand auger, and inserted an iron rod, then pounded the ends flat to assure the rod would not slip out. With that addition, Steffen was able to twirl the weapon at considerable speed, while he remained stationary, holding the shaft over his head with one hand and spinning it with the other.

Walking toward four straw men for practice, the whisper of Steffan's war scythe impressively sliced the air with impunity. He destroyed all the figures in the blink of an eye, as he twirled the weapon, tilting it from side to side. With every practice swing, he saw before him the face of the Turkish aga—Abdul Azim. The Turk's abuse of his wife had continuously festered in his mind, and the result still strained his relationship with Maria.

Wielding the scythe gave him the satisfaction of feeling that someday the war scythe would end the evil Turk's life.

CHAPTER THIRTY

Market Kostel
Spring 1585

After years of planning and hard work, it was time to confront the Castle Lord, for the end of the fifth year drew near. To the distress of Helena and other Am Furtt villagers, they found officials required persuading that planning and preparation were useful and, indeed, needed in the face of the threatened attack.

Helena waited for another market day to confront Count Petar Erdody, as the man strolled through the lanes, just as she had done years earlier. She lay in wait, hidden behind a vendor's stall until the castle gate opened and the Count, his Steward, Captain of the Guard Milic and Bishop Juris walked out through the walls. Other followers also moved through the gate as the morning was warm and the air was fresh with the wafting scent of wheat growing in nearby fields.

The fiefdom nobleman wore no coat, but rather an embroidered cloth vest over a forest-green linen blouse, with an under-tunic beneath of the same color, featuring a hemline trimmed with fur. A belt neatly gathered his clothes around the waist. As was usual, his gray hair fell to his shoulders. The years had added more wrinkles of age to his leather-like face while his dark eyes seemed as cold as ever.

Walking to the center of the market lane as quickly as her frail legs and aged body permitted, Helena stood before the man, blocking his path.

"Eh, who is this woman? Be gone with thee before I call the guards to fetch you away!" the Count demanded. Captain Milic had been walking at the rear of the entourage, but now made his way forward, as did Bishop Juris.

"My Lord," Helena started, doing the best she could to curtsy on legs that were infirm and wobbly. "Perhaps you will remember our previous discussion some years ago, right after the last Turkish attack. We stood right here, outside the castle gate."

Count Erdody was startled. Slowly, it appeared that he recalled the earlier occasion, as his cheeks turned from pasty pale to shades of red.

"Ah, I see that the memory comes back to you, My Lord." Helena continued. "At that time, I asked you to tell the people of Kostel what plans you had to defend the fief the next time the Turkish raiders came to the Kupa Valley. Since then, the serfs of Am Furtt, assisted by our neighbors, have been building our defenses. I know you are aware, as you refused our request to have garrison soldiers help us."

"This is a beautiful morning, and you are again trying to spoil my day, woman. God curse you for that."

Undeterred, Helena continued, "The Turkish commander has vowed to return in five years. As the time is fast approaching, it is again necessary to ask the Lord of Kostel what plans are in place to defend the fiefdom better than the last time."

"Madame, as I recall, I previously said that I do not discuss war plans with serfs and certainly not with a woman." Nodding with a sly smile at his garrison commander, he added, "We have our intentions laid out, and these need not concern you."

Helena had expected an adverse reaction—after all, she was both a woman and one of no breeding in the eyes of the Lord of Kostel. Even so, it was irritating to hear the man dismiss her and all in the fiefdom as being unworthy of even discussing the topic. With great restraint, she kept her voice calm. "I fear Count Erdody those sentiments will not stand, at least not this time. We suffered greatly from the last attack with young ones kidnapped, men scarred by the whip, women abused, storage sheds burned and the hunger and death that followed. And my dear departed husband joined the Lord in heaven above as a result of that attack."

"Again, old woman, your tongue wags incessantly. I follow orders from Vienna, and that means we keep our cannons trained on the main road. Please step aside before I have you thrown into the castle dungeon!"

Just as it had occurred years earlier, a crowd gathered around the two as the combatants traded words. Hundreds of serfs filled the lane, as news of the confrontation spread—Helena from Am Furtt was confronting the Count again.

Looking about her, Helena smiled at the growing throng of people. "May I suggest, My Lord, that you consider another approach?"

"Eh, and what exactly might that be, you silly old woman?"

"Why not appoint Captain Milic and a small group of your subjects as a council to advise you. It allows us to coordinate our communications better and to respond to the attack in an organized manner. It may also produce some suggestions for the benefit of everyone in Kostel facing the evil Turkish soldiers and their brigands."

There were strong murmurs of support from the crowd.

The Count appeared to be flummoxed, standing in the lane, his mouth agape, and his face portraying alternating shades of red. His emotions were not challenging to read, which ranged from extreme fury at someone interrupting his market walk to astonishment at having his authority challenged by one of his serfs. To top it off, it was an old woman standing in his way, and she was being damned insolent and badgering him!

The Count took a step toward the woman, sputtering with emotion. Quickly, the Captain and the Bishop stepped in and restrained him. This was not the place for an overheated reaction.

Captain of the Guard Milic noted, "This old woman has made a useful suggestion, My Lord. Better coordination would be helpful, particularly regarding warning signals and the approach of a Turkish raiding party."

"What say you, My Lord, of this common sense suggestion?" Helena inquired.

"Aye," added the Bishop. "It is a small thing to trade some thoughts regarding a fearsome foe that affects all of us. Why not think on the matter, My Lord, and you can make an announcement on the next market day?"

The castle noble gave every appearance of being off balance, as the whirl of comments seemed to confuse him. Here were his captain and the bishop seemingly agreeing with this old hag, whom the Count apparently thought was an irritating nuisance. Controlling himself with great difficulty, he finally asked, "What is your name, old woman?"

"Helena, Helena Klobucar of Am Furtt. My family has run the toll service at the river crossing and collected your fees for years. My village is also the first place that bears the brunt of any Turkish attack."

"I will think on the matter," the Count said, turning on his heel and quickly walking back through the castle gate.

Steffan gave Captain Milic a tour of the Am Furtt defenses, from the breastworks at the river edge to the enlarged storage shed.

With wonder, the garrison captain listened to the explanation of the killing operation of the twin fists of God. "But how do you know that the spikes will have enough force and momentum to gore both rider and horse?"

"Well, it is based on calculations we have made, and we hope these are correct. We figure the large log, plus the crossbeams and rock, weigh well over one ton. Additionally, each fist has momentum as it falls from the ceiling and swings through its pendulum arc. From that, you can understand how each of these is fearsome for anything or anyone in its path."

"I certainly would not want to be struck by one," the captain acknowledged. "And each is triggered by the levers you pointed out to me; is that right?"

"Yes."

"And how, exactly, do you plan to bait your trap, so the Turks enter this particular shed?"

"Have no fear, Captain; we have already figured that out."

"Impressive. Now, let us again discuss the warning signals."

"And the bowmen you will lend us from the castle guard, Captain," Steffan replied, smiling. "They will be invaluable to assure that some of the brigands continue up the road toward the castle and your cannons."

"Yes, I understand that part of your plan."

"But, may the Good Lord have mercy on me, Captain Milic, I have forgotten my manners? Please accept my apologies! Let us go to my house and sit in the shade, where I have some tasty apricot *rakia*. I assure you that both of us will feel this wondrous liquor sliding down to our gullets and likely continuing to our toes. It will allow us to think more clearly after a couple of glasses."

"Lead on, Steffan Klobucar, I gladly agree with your suggestion and will follow you," the Captain said, smiling broadly.

CHAPTER THIRTY-ONE

Kupa River
May 1585

The Turkish caravan stretched along the dirt road, raising clouds of dust. With a commanding view from a hilltop, Aga Abdul Azim watched, as it snaked on the grassy verge of the river. The day was warm, and the bright sun blazed in the cloudless sky. Tasar led the column of fifteen oxen-pulled wagons, many capable of holding up to eight children.

I vowed to return, Azim mused, *and I kept my word to the whore of Am Furtt.* The thought brought him up short, and he silently berated himself for conjuring up such an ill-conceived opinion. *She is no more a prostitute than I am a lecherous whoremaster*, he concluded.

The sight of his column traveling below him faded as a wash of memories flooded him, and Maria's image filled his thoughts. He realized again that his feelings for her ran deep. Even as he gazed down at his troop, he saw only the memory of her flashing light blue eyes staring at him, framed by her dark hair. For months after their encounter, he dreamed about her nightly, recalling her naked form lying on the straw beside him, her dark devil's triangle set in the fork of her thighs, the swell of her hips and the tapering of her legs.

Last night, she had returned to him in his dreams, opening her arms and nuzzling him against her breast. Then, she had stood and slowly turned around, standing in a shaft of sunlight, exposing the fullness of her dark-haired beauty. *Was it really so magical five years ago,* he wondered *or has time played tricks with my mind? By now, she is probably as broad across her haunches as the backside of my horse,* he imagined, grinning to himself at his dour humor.

Still, it was exciting to remember the pleasure, when he first became a man—having absolute control of a beautiful woman who had to comply with his every wish—his every command. Yes, he had used threats to make her submissive, but that merely heightened the thrill. He longed for some way to recreate their prior experience. Reluctantly, he realized that it was unlikely. Even so, the hopeful thought continued to tantalize him.

I need that vixen in my life! He decided for the hundredth time. *Others hold no interest for me. I am determined to return to Istanbul with both Rado and Maria. Nothing else will satisfy me. Yes, she may resist leaving Kostel and all she has ever known. However, think of the new experiences she will encounter. Allah be praised, can you just imagine her wide-eyed wonder at seeing Istanbul, the largest and most beautiful city of them all.*

Pausing to consider that point, Azim savored a new thought. *Perhaps, she has been waiting for me. Maybe she has even dreamt about the day that I return so we can reunite once more. Could it be that she has pined for me all these years and is anxiously awaiting news of my arrival at this very moment?*

I moved Maria with our lovemaking, particularly following the first time, caressing her ... her hips moved, and she opened herself to me ... I moved her, and I know it ... more than she had ever felt before. When I pressed her afterward, she admitted as much to me. Well, we shall see what my reception will be!

Despite his doubts about Maria, Azim remained supremely confident that he had left the Christian woman in Am Furtt with a child ... a male child, to be exact, named Rado. *Will he be strong, like me?* he wondered. *I hope he has his mother's eyes, for mine are too dark and brooding.* His mind turned to the type of care Rado had received since birth. *She had better have cared for him, or else!* Anger flushed through him at the thought of anyone harming his boy. Calming himself, he smiled at his imagined images of the youngster. Of course, he is walking, talking and already doing chores around the farm—maybe he even milks the family cow. He smiled at the vision. *Once we leave Am Furtt and cross the river, I will set our course straight for Istanbul.*

What will Maria be like, he wondered again, as the image of the peasant woman filled him with overwhelming feelings of anticipation. He was both nervous and excited at the prospect and had never experienced such emotions before. *Why is it not possible that she has missed me?* Azim fanaticized, the expression on his face turning into a sly grin, At that moment, he completely ignored the fact that she had tried to kill him with her eating knife. If possible, his sense of anticipation rose even higher, as he turned his horse downhill to rejoin his group. *We are close to the village and my Maria now!*

With the success of his leadership during the Battle of Torches, Azim had difficulty gaining this assignment that would take him back to the Kupa River and the fiefdom of Kostel for the recurring *devsirme* collection. His Caspian Sea troops returned the previous fall, much to the delight of all to be back in Istanbul. Though the image of Maria Klobucar remained with him and had occupied his dreams for years, he was too embarrassed to share his real reasons for wanting to return to Kostel with his commanding officer, fearing ridicule.

Promotion followed the Persian battle, and Azim's commander considered the *devsirme* assignment below the level of his elevated rank. Even Tasar and Srdoc scratched their heads at their friend's request. Still, Azim prevailed, and he was relieved that he did not have to reveal his real motive to his senior commander.

With a last wistful thought, he shook off his reverie and returned his attention to this assignment. Smiling with self-satisfaction, he thought, *Well, there is no warning bonfire on the hill this time to announce our approach. I assume the Kostelian serfs will not have expected us to cross the Kupa so far west, high up in the mountains, where it begins as a small stream. Then, we traveled eastward, using the river as our guide. Ha, that will teach them.* The expression on his face reflected confident superiority, as he rode downhill toward the caravan.

Azim's troop was much the same as the previous one, with almost fifty men in his entourage. This time, only five Janissaries, including Tasar and Srdoc, accompanied him, along with the usual retinue of slaves to care for the children and perform camp duties. He did have more than two dozen Bosnian irregulars, again headed by Istani. The man was far from the brightest soul, but he did know how to fight and, in the end, Azim figured it was better to know the existing weakness of a man than having it revealed during a battle.

They had gathered several dozen children already, who road in the caged carts. The mindset of the serfs seemed different on this trip. There had been no more attempted bribes from mothers' eager for their sons to become Janissaries, nor for daughters to become handmaidens to wealthy Ottoman overlords. An uneasy feeling tugged at him. As for Istani and others who had raided with him previously, they were looking forward to reaching Kostel, as memories of the Kostelian women filled them with anticipation.

He joined Tazar at the head of the caravan. "Peace be unto thee."

"And you, too, my friend," said his second.

"Is it not unusual that we have seen so few peasants on this journey?"

"It does seem odd, but do not forget, Aga, we come from the west, not the south, and there are fewer farms and settlements this far from the protection of the castles at Market Kostel and Brod na Kupi."

"Quite so," Azim replied. "That is probably the reason."

"So, Aga, are you looking forward to seeing that pretty, blue-eyed woman again, when we reach the village of Am Furtt?"

The question startled Azim. He turned quickly and stared at the short, barrel-chested lieutenant. "What did you say?"

"You know, the pretty one you spent so much time with somewhere out in the fields. I saw you catch up to her, and then you disappeared. I figured you were shedding your virginity between the soft, warm thighs and breasts of that attractive minx."

Embarrassed and blushing, Aga Abdul Azim looked at his second, smiling awkwardly. Then, straightening in the saddle, he said, "Yes, I believe I will look her up again on this trip."

"I am thankful that you did not hold us to our pledge of abstinence when we were last here. Since then, the rules have changed, as we expected, and I am like a liberated man. Did I mention that I have a woman in Istanbul and that I am thinking of marrying her?"

"No, I did not know. I assume that means that you will move out of the barracks. Where will you live?"

"I have found a place on the hillside a few miles from the city. It has space on the ground floor, and we could open a wine shop or perhaps we will sell some of the clothes she makes for other women. I want my own children, not just these that we haul back. I wish for someone to carry my bloodline beyond my time. Do you ever have such thoughts, Aga?"

"It is like you read my mind, Tasar. I, too, wish to have children from my issue—perhaps five or six—hopefully, all boys, who will someday take up duties as a Janissary. I am thirty years old and wish to bounce my progeny on my lap. In fact, I think I left a little package with the blue-eyed wench the last time we were here."

Tasar stared at him in obvious surprise. "How in the name of the Holy Prophet could you know that?"

"Oh, I just have a feeling, and believe it or not, my feelings are just as strong that the little package I left with her is a boy."

"My Aga, you have either become a psychic or ..."

"... a bit touched," Azim finished his thought, laughing. "But, there is no need to lock the door to the barn after the bird has flown ... is there?" he asked.

Both laughed heartily, at the silliness of the remark.

At that moment, Srdoc joined them. "Aga, I have a suspicion that something is wrong, as the map indicates we are close to Brod and Kostel. In my bones, I feel there is danger in this forest."

"Nonsense, these are simple serfs, grubbing out an existence on land owned by someone else, who in turn pays taxes to an emperor located hundreds of miles from here.

Abruptly in the distance, they saw Istani approaching rapidly.

"The way he is galloping his horse, the Bosnian looks like he has a beehive nipping at his behind," Srdoc noted.

As the Bosnian leader skidded his horse to a stop in front of them, a cloud of dust obscured everything. "Aga, Aga, I have something to report," the man said, breathlessly.

Azim asked, "Did you see castle soldiers on the road?"

"No, nothing that definite, but ..."

"What?"

"It is on a tree, Aga."

"What is on a tree?"

"On our side of the river across from Brod, there is a mysterious sign."

"Well, what does it say?" Azim asked. Waiting only a moment, he demanded, "Spit it out!"

"Well ...," the man paused, a confused expression on his face. "It does not say anything. Rather, it is evil looking. My men will see it and think the same as I do. It must be a curse from the dead that has come back to haunt us because of our last raid in this area."

"You are not making much sense, Istani. What, exactly, did you see?"

"It is a warning like a hex from the spirits, casting an evil spell on anyone who gazes upon it."

"Istani," Tasar said in frustration, "in the name of Allah, can you be more precise and tell us what you are talking about?"

"It is a symbol of black magic to me. It has six sides, like spokes of a wheel. Two of these are in the shape of a cross—one right side up and the second upside down."

"It hardly sounds like something that would haunt a man with your experience. And, I would be surprised if your men paid it much attention."

"But, Aga, you do not yet understand. This hex sign has a bleached skull attached in the middle."

"A skull? Bleached white, you say?"

"Yes, my Aga, with an arrow through the openings. You are so worldly. What does it mean? It is a bad sign, is it not? Maybe it is an evil omen from the forest spirits that some of my people still discuss. Perhaps it is a message from one of the little people who live in the Illyrian myths, with their tales of death and the afterlife."

"Nonsense," Azim said. He did not believe in such wild tales. Even so, he knew such ridiculous notions could upset the Bosnian irregulars and set them on edge. He had no desire to see panic among his troops. "Where did you come across this . . . ah, symbol?"

"As I said, Aga, it is painted on several boards nailed to a large tree along the trail."

"So, it can be readily seen as we continue?"

"Yes, Aga."

"Hmm," Tasar noted. "Maybe I was right. Perhaps there is something different about this journey, as compared to the one five years ago. What could these simple serfs be up to?"

"Probably just a trick by some of the village children," Azim responded. "Still, there is no use getting our men riled by such foolishness. Istani, find another route around that area, perhaps along the very edge of the river. Let us keep this to ourselves, and we will let the locals have their little prank of amusement for the moment."

"Whatever you wish, Aga."

As the caravan swung toward the river, the larger town of Brod came into view on the opposite shore, including the fortification. Azim saw Zrinski Castle guards point in their direction, then hurry away to report.

The central tower of the castle was an unusual structure—not a palace or a traditionally shaped castle, but more like an oversized rectangle, sitting on end, reaching a height of forty or fifty feet, with stone battlements surrounding the central core at the lower levels. The oblong tower also housed the living quarters of the castle noble and his family. Yet, the arrow loop openings in the tall structure also gave it an odd look like a childish drawing of a ghostly face.

From the top of the structure, it had a commanding view, including the far side of the river. The last time Azim's company had passed this way, they had been on the other side of the river, and the column had kept its distance from the fortification, well outside the range of the castle's cannons. This time, it was different. Azim saw the large gun pieces run out on the castle walls and soldiers scurried about to load and aim the iron pieces.

"FORWARD, ON THE DOUBLE!" he commanded loudly.

Then, a strange thing happened. Several archers took up positions on the high castle roof, drew their bows and, surprisingly aimed east in the direction of Kostel Castle. Letting loose the flight, the sharp sounds of singing arrows filled the air.

Azim suddenly realized that the peasants had devised a different means to signal the approach of his group and were warning Am Furtt and other hamlets downriver.

Then, arrows began falling among the caravan, as archers swung their longbows toward the Turkish column. By that point, however, most of his men and vehicles were out of range or had fled up the riverbank. Yet, there were several injuries, including two children in one cart, which infuriated Azim.

Riding his horse up the bank to the dirt trail, Azim spurred the animal hard and came around a bend at high speed. At the last moment, he reined in sharply, staring at an ugly, evil-spirit symbol mounted on boards fastened to the trunk of an evergreen tree.

It was just as the Bosnian leader had described—a hexagon with a bleached skull attached in the middle. Unnervingly, the head appeared to be smiling at him, as though spirits of the dead offered their threatening welcome to Azim and his men. He was not a believer in the world of myths; nonetheless, he shivered involuntarily and found the hairs on his arms stiffening. The two crosses on the symbol disturbed him, nagging at something in the back of his mind. *Well, all in the caravan will see this, so there is no use in making more of it than it is. We will pass as though we are on a picnic in the forest*, he thought. Then, he remembered threatening Maria with crucifixion if any harm came to his son, Rado. *Is that what the crosses mean?* he wondered, suddenly feeling less confident.

These questions disappeared, as he heard the thunderous boom of cannons. The soldiers at the castle were firing blind, as trees along the riverbank hid the column. Still, men fought to control frightened animals and their fears. Soon, the cannons stopped, as the troop continued at a quick pace.

Azim breathed a sigh of relief, but it lasted only a moment. He heard the urgent sounds of other whistling arrows in flight but saw none. These flew behind the column, along the route they had just traveled.

Again, Tasar hurriedly rode his horse to Azim's side, an expression of worry on his face. "Quick, something is happening, on the trail we just traveled!"

Turning in his saddle, Azim heard, rather than saw, the loud snapping sounds of tree branches crashing into other limbs, then the thunderous, earth-shaking crash of a massive tree trunk striking the ground, perhaps fifty yards behind them. Immediately, a huge cloud of brown dust rose in the air, obscuring everything in that direction.

"ON ME," Azim shouted to the half-dozen troopers immediately behind him. Hard reining their mounts about, they galloped toward the dust cloud and came to a huge tree lying across the path. Dismounting, Azim made his way around the broad girth of branches. Ax cuts marked the wood, but a large jagged spine stood upright on one side of the stump. The tree's falling momentum had apparently shattered it minutes earlier. Wood chips littered the ground around the tree's base, and Azim noted that many were dried and had turned dark, indicating that cutting the tree had taken place days or, perhaps, weeks earlier.

"Aga, look at these," Srdoc said. He held the ends of thick ropes in his hands.

They continued searching and saw other thick braided cables dangling high up from large trees located close to the fallen one. Tasar noted the curious oddity and said, "This tree was nearly toppled much some time ago. It only remained upright with the aid of these thick hemp ropes. I think they cut the lines only moments ago, letting the weight of the tree pull it down. It seems as though someone does not want us to use this road again!"

"That is quite evident!" Srdoc said. "And look behind you, up the road," he pointed. "See the new dust cloud rising in the air. That is likely a troop of castle riders taking up a position farther back on the trail, to assure that we do not return this way."

"Strange, I saw no evidence of them from the top of the hill," Azim said.

"What does all of this mean?" Tasar asked. "Someone is shadowing our trail, but who would be so foolish? I think we should post a rear guard, in the event the castle soldiers decide to follow us."

"Good idea," Azim said. "We will continue our journey toward Kostel with the main group and the wagons. Have three Janissaries troops take station along this route to determine who is behind us. They are not to engage unless they come under attack. What I want is information. Is that clear?"

"Yes, my Aga. I suggest that we have some of the Bosnian irregulars also remain. The dust cloud we see is of sufficient size to be made by a large patrol."

"I will not engage any enemy until we have better knowledge and intelligence. Besides, I fear the irregulars stir easily and may make too much of the skull and cross symbol."

"Ah, I understand. I will see to it."

"In the meantime, Srdoc, let us keep the caravan moving toward Am Furtt and the castle. I see no need to delay our travels any further. And Tasar, let us send a flight of our own arrows back along the trail we recently traveled so that we, too, can mark it."

Four young peasant boys galloped along the trail that sunny day, dragging large bundles of brush tied to the tails of their horses and creating the dusty illusion that they were a significant force.

Six-year-old Anton rode behind a teenage boy, hugging the older boy's waist to maintain his balance on the horse.

The indiscriminate swarm of Ottoman arrows arched high into the blue sky, falling among the young riders like slivers of death. One struck Anton, tumbling him to the ground.

The boy's companion slid his horse to a stop and threw his leg over the animal's neck to dismount quickly. Raising the younger boy's head, he said urgently, "Anton, speak to me. Please, say something!"

Anton, the heir to the Klobucar hide in the village of Am Furtt, died instantly from his wound that day.

CHAPTER THIRTY-TWO

Azim directed ten men to split off to secure the ferry. He well remembered the last trip, and he wanted to assure that his troop had a means of crossing the river when they turned south. For the time being, the carts, slaves and the main body of the caravan remained well back along the trail, but out of range of the Zrinski Castle cannons. With the remaining men, Azim rode toward the village, but he slowed the column's pace, as smoke rose ahead.

Rounding a bend, he saw the last flaming arrows land, igniting the straw and kindling mixture, setting a roadblock on fire. He noticed another sign and skull mounted on a wooden post.

At the edge of the village, the troop reined in. "Istani, take your men toward Fara and begin capturing more young ones. Tasar, Srdoc and I will see what other mischief these Am Furtt serfs have in mind, and we will hand some of them their heads to reward their efforts."

"As you wish," the Bosnian leader said. He wheeled his horse and motioned to his men with his sword to follow him.

The three Janissaries continued into the village but suddenly pulled up. From the direction of the road leading to Fara, they heard screams coming from the Bosnian group, as arrows found their marks from archers hidden in the recesses of outbuildings and the forest.

"I hope Istani knows enough to double back if need be," Srdoc said, "and to cut through the fields to avoid going too close to the cannons at the castle."

"Surely, he will remember that those guns cover the road to Gottschee," Tasar noted, wiping the sweat from his brow on that warm and brightly lit morning.

"Aga, look," Tasar said, pointing. A distant shed had a larger image of the mystical image painted on the side, with the words, "RADO IS HERE."

Azim's heart leaped at the thought that his son was so close. Involuntarily, a shiver ran through him. He also realized that this was an obvious place for a trap. "These farmers want to play games of war, do they?" he said to his companions. "Well, we Janissaries surely can teach them a thing or two and the right way to do it."

Srdoc's lopsided smile tugged at his face, creating an evil smirk, and Tasar's grin reflected the man's urge for a good fight.

They walked their horses toward the shed in silence, vigilantly glancing about with their swords unsheathed.

"If my eyes do not deceive me, Aga, the storage shed looks newer and larger than the others," Tasar noted. As they neared the structure, he added, "It is much bigger and considerably taller, too."

Azim nodded, and said, "It is an odd shape and leads me to wonder how the serfs use it. I do not recall if we burned it when we were last here, but it must have been destroyed, for this structure has been rebuilt recently."

The three stopped at a wide entrance. Azim swung one booted leg over the pony's withers and dropped to the ground while his companions remained mounted and vigilant.

Gazing into the interior, Azim said, "It is dark inside, but I see two other entrances. One is on the right side, and another is directly across from this opening. Both are large enough to allow a team and loaded wagon to drive through—or a mounted horseman."

Srdoc noted, "It seems unusually quiet. Maybe it is not a trap."

"Well," Azim said, "we are Janissaries, and we will show these poor, uneducated serfs how battles and wars are fought by us, the victors of the Battle of Torches. Tasar, you take the side opening and enter first. That will give Srdoc time to reach the door at the other end, and he can follow you. If the two of you flush out any 'serf warriors,'" he continued disdainfully, "I will deal with them at this entrance, as they fly out like hens fleeing a chicken coop before the snapping jaws of a fox."

Tension filled the air. If possible, the evil smile on Srdoc's face broadened, and Tasar's horse pawed the ground nervously.

"Off with you," Azim commanded, "and may Allah protect you."

He watched his two lieutenants walk their horses around the corner of the large shed. His doorway had two swinging doors, which were both open. He peered inside, but he distinguished little, as his eyes were still adjusting from bright sunlight to the dim interior. Then, he saw the head of Tasar's horse at the side entrance to his right. With a loud war cry, his second in command spurred the animal with the heels of his boots and charged into the darkened interior, sword stretched forward in the classic attack style.

Suddenly, the entire wooden structure of the building seemed to move and sway, accompanied by unbelievably loud, high-pitched screeches of wood heavily chafing against wood. A whoosh of air indicated something big was moving inside the shed.

Watching Tasar and his horse, Azim was at first surprised and then shocked, as a huge log swung down from the ceiling at his end of the building, traveling at a high rate of speed. Tasar looked left, and his eyes widened, but before he could react, sharp stiletto spikes impaled him and his horse. There was only a muted grunt from the big burly man, whose sword clanged to the ground. The horse emitted a wild and loud, unnatural animal scream, like a strangled shriek, as the force of the big killing machine swung through its arc of death, physically lifting both man and beast into the air.

Azim's astonishment continued, as he watched the log return in its pendulum arc. He could tell that his friend and the horse were dead, as the bodies dragged along the shed's dirt floor, slowing and finally stopping the weapon. After a moment, Tasar and his mount, muscles twitching in spasms of death, slithered off the long metal stilettos, with unnervingly eerie suction-like noises, as the long sharp spikes exited the disemboweled horse and man. Both dropped to the ground in a rapidly growing pool of blood. A cloud of acrid, blue friction smoke added to the bizarre scene, and the smells of death inside the storage shed were pungent.

Azim's face turned white with the shock and realization that his friend was dead— instantly killed by the trickery and treachery of the Am Furtt serfs.

Suddenly, Srdoc was at the door opposite him, staring at Tasar in the middle of the shed and the long spiked arm hanging from the ceiling.

Azim opened his mouth to shout a warning, but Srdoc, sword raised high, gave his cry of battle and hurtled into the interior. As he passed the entrance, a shadow shifted to his right. Instinctively, Srdoc slashed down with his sword, while continuing into the darkened shed to confront anyone who dared to challenge him.

Once more, the building trembled and added horrific screeches to the pungent smells of burning grease and wood permeating the shed's interior. Srdoc had only an instant to see the danger swinging toward him from his right side. The tall man turned in the saddle at the first sound and classically raised his sword toward the danger, as the swinging weapon of death moved swiftly toward him. He managed to cry out, "Allah is . . .," only to have his words end abruptly by the thudding impact of the tree trunk striking flesh and bone. Skewered by multiple spikes, the log's momentum lifted the big man out of his saddle and swung him high toward the ceiling before returning him to the shed's floor; after a moment, he, too, dropped off the spikes near the body of Tasar.

Srdoc died instantly, a frozen expression of surprise on his face, while an odd ray of sunshine, filtering in through the spaced sidewalls, strangely highlighted the scar on the right side of the man's face. The violence of the collision knocked the Turk's horse down, but it immediately bounded to its feet, uninjured, and it bolted straight at the opening where Azim stood guard.

He threw himself violently to the side, and just managed to avoid the sharp hooves of the terrified animal. Getting to his feet, he again looked around the inside of the shed. And there she was—Maria. After all the intervening years, she was standing against the wall to the left of his entrance, her hand on some form of control. *That must have triggered at least one of these massive killing machines,* Azim surmised. He watched her untie her apron from around her waist and stand very still for an instant. Despite the dim light in the shed, her face was lit by the sun. He recalled her naked form turning before him in a similar patch of light, five years earlier.

She glanced at him with a penetrating glare that was stone cold, with her blue eyes set in a face flushed with fury.

Still, it sent a shiver of delight and anticipation through him to see her again. Her backside had not broadened, he quickly noted, and her figure was nicely rounded and full breasted, with her hair pulled back under a black babushka. She looked as beautiful as he remembered.

"You are a murdering *kučkin sin!*" she shouted at him. "You have returned, but you will not get away this time."

It was an ominous warning, yet Azim's elation was such at seeing the love of his life and hearing her voice again, that the threat of her words escaped him and, momentarily, the loss of his two lieutenants was forgotten.

Maria hurriedly ran past the destructive weapons and gruesome carnage to the other side of the shed. Only then did Azim see another woman, an older one, lying on the ground, still clutching a young boy in her arms. Maria knelt, hugging the boy, and then turned to the other woman. "Nana, where are you hurt?" she asked, her voice panicked. Turning the unmoving woman onto her side, a spurt of blood pulsated from a sharp-edged sword-wound. Maria pushed her apron against it, trying to stem the flow from the neck wound.

Azim, still confused and stunned by the swiftly moving events, stared in horror at the bodies of his compatriots lying in the dirt, as he warily walked toward Maria. A deep feeling of regret arose in him at the loss of his friends and comrades. *They were real men who followed me into major battles,* he thought, *only to lose their lives on a routine devsirme assignment. After their heroic and courageous roles at the Battle of Torches, each could have taken duties that were more prestigious and reflective of their skills. They had ridden with me out of a sense of unity and loyalty, only to end up dead on the dirt floor of a drying shed in this miserable village.* An overwhelming feeling of sadness shrouded him, as he continued to walk toward the two women and the boy on the far side of the building while looking about, alert for more surprises and traps—perhaps from Maria's husband.

"Nana, do not leave me," Maria wailed. Lifting the woman's head and holding it in her lap, Maria caressed her cheeks and brushed the matted hair from her forehead.

As he approached, Azim could see that the woman was doomed, as arterial blood surged from her neck. He stopped several feet away.

With eyelids fluttering, the white-haired woman's eyes opened and her lips compressed into a tight smile. "My child," she whispered hoarsely, "you are more deserving than me when I became Petar's wife." She stopped, closing her eyes for a moment. "Men think it is their world, and we let them pretend. You and I know that it is the woman's place to run the house, and if necessary, the farm ... even the village sometimes, eh?" she said, coughing. "And, we control the money, my dear," attempting a small smile again.

"Nana, lie still, here in my arms! Do not try to talk."

"No, my time has come. You, Maria, pay the castle taxes but see that you hold some back. You also account for the tolls. Again, slide some coins into a side pocket. Always remember that your two first duties are to support Steffan and to pick a proper wife for your eldest son.

They remained silent for a moment, as the woman gasped for breath. "Maria, promise me that you will pray for me so that I can pass through purgatory. I want to rejoin

Petar and sit with our Lord as quickly as I can. Promise me!"

"Of course, I will."

"I always knew you were the right one for my grandson." The old woman closed her eyes as a final breath escaped her.

CHAPTER THIRTY-THREE

Overcome with sadness, Maria bent over Helena and wept, as Rado squirmed, trapped between the two women. Sitting her son down next to the wall, Maria placed her apron over Helena's face and slowly rose.

Azim seemed unsure. Tentatively, he asked, "Maria, is that Rado, our son?"

Slowly turning her head, Maria's tearful expression was full of loathing. In a full-throated voice that cracked with emotion, she replied, "No, this is not your son. This is Rado Klobucar, and he is my son. No one, not you or your barbarians can take him from me. Not even Mathias, the former son of a Christian man and woman, now turned murderer for a corrupt empire, will take him from me."

Smiling broadly at the news of his son, Azim still held his sword, as he looked over his shoulder to scan the darkened interior again for other possible dangers. "So, Maria, I was right. I did leave you a package, and it turned out to be a boy, just as I predicted—not bad for a virgin beginner, eh? He will become a great Janissary warrior one day."

"You smug bastard—five years has not changed your arrogance!"

Still looking around the shed, Azim said grudgingly, "I compliment you and your people on the planning behind your defenses. From my years of military experience, the twin swinging arms delivered death with surprising effectiveness, and neither of my men had any opportunity at all, despite their many years of battle experience."

"As always, you have ears but refuse to use them. No one will take Rado from this village!"

Azim stared at the boy in the dim light but seemed unable to distinguish many features. Given the deaths of his two lieutenants, the Turkish aga continued to be suspicious and uneasy. He turned slowly in a circle to take in the full interior of the shed. As he faced her once more, he said, "So, Maria, who is to stop me, from taking my son to Istanbul?"

"You are the lowest form of animal. I will kill him and myself before I allow it, you godless killer of innocent people!"

"She will not, but I will," a young man said, stepping through a door and out of the dark shadows on the far side of the shed.

Azim turned quickly in the direction of the voice. "And who do we have here? Are you some kind of serf warrior?"

"We met once before when you had me flogged. I am Steffan, Maria's husband."

His appearance seemed to startle Azim, as he stared at the younger man.

Comparing the two, Maria noted that her husband was shorter than the Turk was, yet both had broad shoulders and each looked powerfully built. Steffan was stockier while Azim's waist was narrower. The Muslim dressed in flowing, brightly colored robes. Steffan, leaning jauntily on his war scythe, wore coal-black clothes, top to foot, with tightly fitted linen attire, from the strapped hat on his head to his linen-bound leggings.

Steffan continued, "I am sorry that I missed the weapons performing their duty on your men. We call them the fists of God. It took us years to build them, but I can see from the slaughter that they did their job well, and apparently missed disemboweling only one horse—and of course, you. I was called away to make sure that your other men at the ferry crossing and those on the road to Fara came to the same ending that is in store for you."

"Steffan," Maria blurted out, "one of the soldiers struck Nana with his sword! She died moments ago in my arms."

For the first time, the young man noticed the old woman, who lay crumpled on the shed floor. He uttered an animal-like growl—part anger and part hate. His blazing stare returned to Azim. "Your evil ways vilify everything touched by you and your men," he said emotionally, tears clouding his eyes. "First, it was my *Stari* that you killed during the last raid, now my Nana. Never, ever, will you leave Kostel alive," he said, his voice cracking with emotion and fury. "Of that, you can be certain. Even now, you are drawing your last breaths!"

Out of concern for Steffan, Maria continued, "It was not this Turk who did it, but one of his men!"

"It makes no difference! They are all under the command of this devil, and he takes his orders from the foulest empire that man has ever devised!"

"Simply one of the tragedies of conflicts these days," Azim said, in a voice that was even, but flat and lacking in sympathy.

Gathering himself and wiping away the tears from his cheeks, Steffan spoke in a guttural voice. "We are not violent people like you. However, you can see the changes from prior years, when we just accepted the tragedies inflicted by you and your men."

"Brave talk is as elusive as puffs of smoke. Deeds are what count in this world when it comes to fighting."

Ignoring Azim words, the young man continued, "Speaking of tragedies and a proper ending, you Turkish bastard, you may not have noticed the deep pit we dug outside on the far side of this shed. We access it through the wide door you see over there—the one I used to enter the shed. After I kill you, we will drag the bodies of you, your men and the horse to the pit. Then, we will fill the hole with *drek* from our pigs and cows. In a few years, the manure will naturally putrefy and ferment, until even the bones crumble. Only then will your life and the others have a purpose, as we spread the mixture to fertilize our fields. That will be your fate, Turkish commander. A pile of *drek* will mark the end of your life, and the same pile will be your headstone. Nice to contemplate, is it not? I think it is most fitting for those who kidnap children and destroy the lives of others."

Maria noticed a slight shudder as the Turkish commander contemplated Steffan's words, despite the man's rigid self-control. Worried about what would happen next, she clutched Rado and backed against a wall.

Breaking the silence, Azim asked, "What are you holding, farmer? It looks like a black stick with two blades."

"It is a war scythe," Steffan answered crisply, the red flush of anger on his face. "Scythes are tools we serf farmers know very well," he continued, as tears of sorrow continued rolling down his cheeks.

"Huh! Well, let us stop talking and see how well that black pole of yours works," Azim said, positioning his blade forward.

"Stop," Maria screamed, leaving her son by the side of the shed. "Halt this evil right now! Mathias, do you want

Rado to watch the two of you kill yourselves, right here on the land where it all began?"

Both men stopped at the outburst and turned toward her.

"Mathias, you can see that we have organized resistance to the tactics of terror used by you and your Turkish brigands. We serfs are no longer prepared to see our children kidnapped and made slaves to your Sultan and the evil ways condoned by your religious leaders. Even now, the young ones you stole on this journey are free. Your remaining fighting men are galloping up the road toward the castle, where the guards will cut them to ribbons with their long guns. Our bowmen at the river crossing have already disposed of the force you sent there. The Ottoman reign of terror for this stretch of the Kupa River is over. You are a man with a warrior's mind. Clearly, you can sense the change!"

"Ha, it is over only when Sultan Murad says that . . ."

"Oh my God! For once, shut up and stop talking like the ass-end of a horse. Go save your remaining men."

"Not without my son. He is too precious to me. He will carry my seed into the future. You recall that I predicted his birth. I will not leave without him. And, Maria, dear, you *too* will return to Istanbul with me."

She was shocked at the Turk's words. Slowly, as if dazed, she replied, "Me—travel with you to Istanbul? You are as mad as a rabid skunk running in crazed circles, Mathias! I despise you! Seeing you again, and your presence in my village, is repulsive to me. I could not think of anything worse than being a part of your world and your religion, which permits such butchery and kidnapping. I would rather throw myself into the river and drown than be associated with you, as what—I guess they would call me a white plaything for a white slave—a concubine that you could do with as you wish? Leave us alone, you bastard, while you still have a chance of atoning for your evil ways."

"When I leave, Rado is coming with me. Of that, I am sure."

"NEVER," Maria shouted.

"Who will stop me," the Turk snapped.

"Aga Abdul Azim," Steffan said gruffly, his voice filled with fury, "you will have to face me first, and my serf war scythe, for my son and wife go nowhere with you. Further, the deaths of my grandparents cry out for revenge."

"Of course, you boorish peasant," Azim responded, fully turning toward the younger man. "It will be good for the boy to see his father, a Janissary warrior, win in battle, without stooping to surprises and underhanded tricks, like those that killed my men.

Maria trembled with fear for Steffan and clutched Rado closer.

Suddenly, the whooshing sound of the twirling war scythe filled the air, as Steffen hefted the twin-bladed weapon above his head and spun it rapidly, holding the centered metal pin in the shaft and tilting the spinning blades toward the Turk.

Azim gave ground just in time, avoiding the sharp point of the first blade. In the next instant, the curved second blade confronted him, as the young man spun the shaft swiftly while slowly walking toward him.

She saw that Azim was as nimble as a cat in avoiding the twin blades. He also seemed to be assessing the threat posed by Steffan.

His sword came down hard on the scythe's third pass, which lowered the blade to calf-height. The Turk jumped over the next spin to avoid losing a leg as Steffan also stepped over the spinning war scythe.

"Well, come on, Janissary captain or general, or whatever the hell you are," Steffen called out, scornfully. "Are we to fight, or are you just going to keep leaping like a cow with a blowfly up her arse?" He stopped and cockily leaned on his staff again, a fiercely contemptuous expression on his face.

Even in the dimly lighted shed, Maria noted the sheen of sweat on her husband's face and realized the effort it took to wield his new weapon.

Azim charged to deliver a killing blow, his sword held high.

Ready, and light on his feet, Steffan switched tactics, twirled the shaft rapidly and then surprisingly, he moved quickly and directly at the Turk.

Azim nearly encountered the descending point of a curved blade, as it passed a mere fraction of an inch in front of his chest. Again reacting swiftly, Azim hastily backed out of the shed's doorway and into the bright sunlight.

Steffan, blinking and squinting in the bright sunlight, followed him, twirling the war scythe above his head.

Maria saw that her husband's quick reaction and the reach of his weapon prevented Azim from closing on him. *The Turk must know many sword-wielding tactics as an experienced and battle-tested soldier,* she thought. *I pray Steffan can keep him at a distance.* She realized that her husband's substantial effort to wield the weapon might wear him down and give the evil Turk a deadly opening. She watched him spin it again, and once more advance on the Turk.

After avoiding several more passes of the blades, Azim brought the full weight of his well-condition physique and the heft of his sword across the wooden handle, driving the younger man and the shaft against the frame of the shed's stout doorway. Black chips of wood scattered from the collision of metal and rock-hardened wood, startling both men, as the muscles in their arms trembled from the force of the blow.

Recovering first, Azim crouched low and thrust his blade at Steffan's leg.

Steffan jumped away easily and backed into the shed, his face covered in sweat. Then, he took the offensive once more, spinning the weapon.

Azim gave ground and retreated into the sunlight once more. Catching his foot on a stone, he tripped and fell backward.

Maria felt as though her heart was in her throat, thinking this was the end of the evil Turk and the battle.

At the last moment, Azim turned on his side to avoid a blade that came down and buried itself in the dirt inches from his shoulder. Jumping up quickly, the soldier brought down the flashing blade of his sword on the wooden shaft, aiming for the same place as before.

Once more, chips flew, and both men heard the crack of splitting wood, as the sword struck the scythe a mighty blow, slamming the end to the ground. Reacting instinctively, Azim swiftly raised the sword over his head and brought it down once more with all of his strength, splintering the handle in two. With that, the Turk charged furiously, driving Steffan into the shed and the dim interior.

Still clutching Rado, Maria screamed with fear.

Steffan had no choice—he hurriedly backed into the darkened shed, with one-half of his weapon in each hand. Dropping one end, he grasped the remaining staff in his right hand and adopted the classic scythe swing of winding up his body and pulling the cutting blade through the air with all his strength—and missed the charging Turk.

Instantly, Azim pushed him against an upright support post and held his sword horizontally against her husband's throat, pinning him.

Steffan dropped the broken scythe and stretched himself taller, standing on his toes, while trying to keep his chin and throat above the sharp edge of the blade.

Through parched lips, Azim jeered, "Do you see, you peasant fool, this is how a trained soldier fights and overcomes his enemy." Slowly he moved the sharp edge of the sword a fraction of an inch, drawing a trickling line of blood. "The contempt in my eyes will be the last thing that you will see before I slice off your head! When I finish here, I will take *my son* and *your wife* to Istanbul.

"Drek!"

"You pretend to be a warrior! Ha! I will cut you nice and slow, very slow, so you can feel every inch of my long blade cutting your jugular while your body pumps out your life's blood. It is nice to contemplate, is it not?" he snarled with a guttural snort.

Suddenly, the smirk on Azim's face changed, replaced by an expression of unbelievable pain, and then agony, as the sharp point of a scythe blade drove through his left shoulder and beyond, affixing him to the post and just missing Steffan.

"No, Mathias," Maria hissed in his ear, "today it is your day to die. Go to your Prophet and Allah. There, you will be happy. The last thing *you* will see is the blazing hatred in my blue eyes for the sins you and all of your people have committed, and the tragedy you Turks have inflicted upon us with your *devsirme*. Today, it is your turn to pay as we collect our tax in blood!"

Steffan managed to push the sharp edge of the sword away from his neck with his bare hands, freeing himself. With bleeding hands, he reached behind to his waistband and drew out a dagger. With a fierce thrust, Steffan drove it to the hilt into the Turk's lower back, and then violently twisted it. "That is how we kill our pigs," he shouted, his voice echoing triumphantly in the darkened shed.

"Maria, my first love," Azim whispered hoarsely, "I moved you ... and you felt it ... was there never a time ... even a moment ... when you had deep feelings for me?" he gasped.

"Yes," she hissed through clenched teeth, her face inches from his.

Then, bending over, she picked up the remaining half of the war scythe. "Yes, Mathias, I have those feelings for you right now, for our Lord, Jesus Christ, tells us to love thy enemy, bless those who curse us, do good to them that hate and pray for those who spitefully use us. Your life represents all of these sins. Thus, as my enemy, I will do as the Lord says and love your memory, and I will pray for your miserable soul although it will likely reside in the Devil's boiling caldron somewhere in a dungeon-like cave deep in the bowels of Hell!"

Stepping back, she swung the other scythe handle with all of her strength and buried the sharp end of the pike in the center of his back.

"Maria!" Azim screamed in anguish. For a brief moment, he managed to turn his face slightly and look into her eyes.

Watching, she said the words first spoken by John the Baptist, "He that loveth not, knoweth not God, for God is love."

Azim shuddered, convulsed by pain. Then, the light faded from his dark brown eyes, silencing the Turkish commander, Aga Abdul Azim, forever.

CHAPTER THIRTY-FOUR

Saint George's Day
Market Kostel
<u>1694</u>

Johannes Stanislaus, the Storyteller, paused. Tears fell from his blue eyes, dampening his whiskered cheeks, as the plucking of the strings continued. The audience was silent at the thought of the courage required to defeat the Turkish attack and Maria and Helena's bravery. In his singsong style, the old man continued.

> On my father's knee
> I heard him say,
> Be damned, sultan
> Thrice be damned
> For thee is evil.

> You shackle the old
> Steal our children
> Parents weep and wail.
> Long do I cry, for next,
> It will be my son.

The gusle stilled. Those gathered around the knoll were subdued, as the story's ending affected the crowd's mood. "Maria's heroism became renowned. At a later time, I will sing her story to you—perhaps at your festival in the new year. The village of Am Furtt took on importance, as indeed, did all in the Fiefdom of Kostel. The serfs had taken a stand. Additionally, they had succeeded against heavy odds.

"Yet, Maria thought that she and Steffan faced a last difficult challenge, the loss of Anton. The entire fiefdom came together at the cemetery in Fara for the young boy's funeral. In the fief's resistance to the attack, there were three casualties, including the boy's death. Everyone mourned.

"One evening, as Maria and Steffan watched the sunset from the side of the tollhouse building, she finally found the courage to raise the issue that festered inside her. Dressed in black mourning clothes, she pressed her head against her husband's shoulder and whispered, 'I am so sorry to have brought such troubles to our family.'"

"Almost rudely, he pushed her away, looking into her upturned face. 'Do not take upon yourself that which you have not caused. Your defense of Anton was unbelievably brave. Nana said to me that I would never find another woman like you again; nor a better mother for our young Rado. And, Maria, I honestly believe that she was right.'"

"'That is my concern, Steffan,' Maria answered. 'There no longer is a direct bloodline from the Klobucar family, running through to young Rado. I worry about the doubts you will have in the future, even though I know we plan to have more children. Heaven knows, we will need more hands to help us with the farming tasks. And, most importantly, the eventual transfer of the hide from father to son passes to the eldest, and now that Anton is gone . . .'" Maria's sad voice trailed off and stopped.

"At that, blessed Kostelians," Johannes said, "Steffen broke into a thunderous laugh that stunned the woman. Tears of mirth came to the young man's eyes before he calmed himself sufficiently to explain. 'Do not misunderstand—I mourn the loss of our Anton. He will forever remain in our hearts. But as to lineage, Petar and Nana calculated that the families in this area have been living here for hundreds of years. They lived generation after generation, in the same farming hamlets, many in the same houses—surviving, working, marrying and having babies on this narrow bench of farmland along the Kupa River. After so long,' he continued, 'it would be amazing, even unbelievable, if all of us do not have at least a tiny share of everyone else's family line in us.'"

"Smiling with happiness, Maria was pleased. She buried her face against her husband's shoulder."

The teller of tales concluded, in his singsong voice—

> I heard long ago
> And tell in this way
> For all to know

The gusle stopped for the last time, and the white-haired man stood slowly and bowed to the crowd.

They clapped, cheered and shouted with joy, to thank Johannes Stefanich, the favorite storyteller in the Kupa River Valley.

AUTHOR'S NOTES

In the 1990s, I became interested in collecting family stories, which ultimately led me into genealogy to track repetitive names, as well as spelling variations used over the centuries. I had success on my father's side of the family tree, but I came to blank walls in tracing my mother's side across the Atlantic—particularly her mother, Katherine. Through years of trial and error and using a wide variety of search techniques, I finally found her listed on the Ellis Island immigration records, despite an unimaginable spelling of her surname. Eagerly scanning the ship's officer's written entries, I found answers to the many questions listed under column headings that extended across two large-size pages—Age on arrival-19; Marital status-M; Date of arrival-October 5, 1902; Ethnicity-Hungarian (all emigrants at the time from the Austro-Hungarian Empire were entered as Hungarian or Austrian). Her place of residence was listed as Puce. *PUCE?*

The last answer baffled me. I could not be sure of the spelling. I assumed it was a town or village, but I did not know its location or country. No living relative could answer the question of her birthplace although some said that she spoke Croatian with a Slovenian accent. Others speculated that she had been born in Brod na Kupi, Croatia, the town located on the river dividing present-day Croatia and Slovenia.

Still, the town or village of "Puce" remained a mystery for some years. Hence, finding the Catholic Church parish for the area and the records still in its vault were unknown possibilities. In desperation, I joined a Slovenian chat site, asking for help. Within a day, a response arrived, requesting that I send an image of PUCE from the immigration record. I complied and within days, the man responded. He told me:

1. The correct name is Pierce (pronounced Pir-ch-e), a farming village in Slovenia.
2. It sits a few miles from the parish church in the village of Fara.
3. Both hamlets were part of the former fiefdom of Kostel.
4. He had completed his doctoral thesis on this very fief—in English.
5. And, he asked if I would like a copy. Sometimes you have to be lucky.

After years of research, it felt as though I had struck the mother lode. However, that was not all—part of his doctoral research included translating castle tax records, extending back to the 16th century. With such material, plus the *Status Animarum*, parish priests' records, it was possible to trace Katherine's ancestry back to the 16th century. Lastly, he asked if I would like his help in performing the task. Yes, it truly was the mother lode!

I began my research and education on the former fiefdom of Kostel and the village of Am Furtt (translation—river crossing—and one of the several previous names for the rural hamlet of Pirce). It exists today following several name changes, and the Klobucar surname is historically accurate. These provide the location and family name of the fictional characters used in the novels.

Catholic Church and castle tax documents contain both family names and the hamlet, some dating back to the sixteenth century. No one with the Klobucar surname currently resides in the village. It turns out that these ancestors were serfs—in servitude to the Lord of the Castle—slaves tied to the *never* changing land, in the same small hamlet and lived at the same house address—No. 7—as far back as written records exist—for nearly five centuries.

The man who assisted me was Dr. Stanislav Južnič.

His work along with other extensive research became the informational foundation for the novels in the "K" series.

Derbent, Russia

The major and minor ranges of the Caucasus Mountains are nearly seven-hundred miles long, ranging from northwest to southeast and stretching from the shores of the Black Sea to the Caspian Sea, except for a narrow mile and one-half wide strip of land at the city of Derbent. Today, it is located in the Republic of Dagestan, the largest southernmost Russian city.

From one hundred feet below sea level, at the edge of the Caspian, elevations rise rapidly, with peaks soaring to eighteen thousand feet, as the Arab and Eurasian tectonic plates collide.

Historically, there are many chapters in the continuing wars and battles for control of Derbent. In the eighth century, the Persian *Sassanid* rulers began building the mighty fortress around the perimeter of the town, requiring trading caravans to pass through the city gates to traverse the Caucasus Mountains. It was an ideal situation for collecting tolls from passing Silk Road caravans. Many regional powers coveted the fort through the centuries, captured it and then lost control. Included were the Romans (more than once), the Byzantine Empire, Tamerlane's Mongols, the pre-Islamic Persian Sassanid Empire and the Ottoman Empire. It first came under Russian control with the territorial expansion of Peter the Great. The present Persian name translates to "narrow gates."

The oldest structure in the city is a mosque from the seventh century, built over a Christian church that dates to the sixth century. Other archeological finds in the area are over five thousand years old. In the ninth century, the Caliph Harun al-Rashid lived in the city, along with a population of fifty thousand. Historians note that Movses Kaghankatvatsi, an Armenian author, first described the fort in the 10th Century, in his historiographical work, *The History of the Country of Albania*. Later, Kirakos of Gandzak also referred to it in his 13th Century work, *History of Armenia*.

Devsirme

Turkish Sultans distrusted their noblemen and tribal leaders, both in the administration of the growing expanse of territories and in matters of war. To counter their power and influence, Murad I established the Janissaries, which became an elite troop of warriors, whose loyalty was only to the Sultan. Initially, the corps was comprised of captured enemy soldiers and the forced enlistment of conquered people, such as those living on the Anatolia Peninsula of Asia Minor (a significant part of the present-day Turkey). Over time, the Sultan and his advisors found these sources inadequate for various reasons. They also dismissed using slaves from Africa. Their answer lay in kidnapping pre-puberty children, mostly Christian, as white slaves. By molding and teaching these youngsters, the Sultan's ambitions succeeded in creating a new class of people who became warriors and administrators within his Empire.

The Qur'an, the Islamic holy book, and the words of Muhammad prohibit slavery. Despite the contradiction, policy interpretations of Islamic text contained in fatwas issued by Islamic scholars, or muftis, excluded the practice of slavery for only those who followed Islam, while permitting the enslavement of people from other religions, referred to as "nonbelievers."

"Devsirme" is the Turkish word for "gathering or collecting," much as a shepherd gathers his flock—and became the name for the program to capture white slaves. Turkish raiders "harvested" the strongest and fairest five-to-ten-year-old children at periodic intervals of four to five years, traveling the countryside, particularly lands occupied by Christians. The captured children made the long journey to the largest city in Europe, Istanbul, located on the Sea of Marmara, at the tip of the Golden Horn. The captives converted to Islam, learned the language and became skilled in one of the several disciplines. It was a miserable lot for Christian families to pay the price of the tragic arrangement with the blood of their kin—their children. Raids by Turkish regular soldiers and Muslim brigands regularly occurred between the 15th and 17th centuries. Over the years, some scholars estimate that the total number of white slaves captured stands at over one million. The practice finally ended following World War I.

Greek Fire

The development of the incendiary weapon dates to the seventh century by the Byzantine Empire. Typically, it found use in sea battles, as flames continued burning while floating on water. Historians say it was a deciding factor in some conflicts, including two Arab sieges of Constantinople, thus saving the Byzantine Empire.

For hundreds of years, it was a secret weapon with the composition of the combustible liquid known only to a few; it was so secret that the formula and originator have been lost to antiquity. In sea battles, they ejected the oil under intense pressure through a siphon mounted on a specialized ship or galley.

Many believe that the liquid was probably some form of refined petroleum, comparable to modern napalm. The terrifying fiery substance stuck to almost any surface. Only sand or vinegar, and surprisingly, urine extinguished the flames.

Oral Tradition

Written languages developed throughout the ages, but only a few flourished and continued to modern times. Many became victims of wars, natural disasters or difficult formats (chiseled stone tablets, for example). Most faded into antiquity.

In stark contrast, humans have used the oral tradition to pass on stories of bravery and life experiences, a practice that has continued for thousands of generations to this day. At one time, traveling storytellers, or bards, moved between villages and towns, generationally passing along myths and legends, using traditional oral recitation. The teller—part historian, teacher and entertainer—altered words and made stylistic changes to a story (poem) with each presentation, tailoring it to the interest of the audience. Even so, a story continued its central thematic basis.

Researchers have sought to understand how story lines remained consistent through many recitations, narrated by countless tellers and repeated over a multiplicity of generations. An example of the difficulty in keeping original story lines intact is the parlor game that involves whispering a phrase into the ear of the first in a line of people, who, in turn, does the same, until the last one speaks the phrase aloud. Everyone is surprised that the phrase changed in the retelling. Linguistic research indicates that using formulas within "the context of poetic verse" produces consistency. Researcher Alfred Lord defines it as "almost mathematical" in form and provides rigidity to the story, even after the narrator tailors it for an audience. An often-cited example is the many versions of the great flood (Noah's Flood), which is thousands of years old and is found throughout ancient civilizations and languages.

In Ryan and Pitman's book, *Noah's Flood*, summary research findings of Serbo-Croatian storyteller examples show that "...for a myth of yore to survive unscathed from repeated recitation, it needs a compelling story, a narrative of human history from its origins to the present." Further, it needs to be "persuasive, especially when interleaved with significant events that might be interpreted as the random whims of the supernatural gods or deserved punishment ... leading to a heroic struggle for survival. Oral tradition tells such stories."

Secondly, within the context of families, the oral history continues with the retelling of stories generation after generation. The tradition is present in almost every culture. From elder family member to youngest, these, too, pass from one generation to the next, and the oral tradition is likely the greatest ongoing legacy of repeated recitation and a universal teaching technique.

Silk Roads

The four thousand-mile-long trade routes began in the 3rd century B.C., during the Han Dynasty in China. Trade goods journeyed west, comprising spices, salt, clothing, aromatics, paper, rugs, metal pots and, particularly, silk. There were three main east-to-west routes, collectively known as the Silk Roads. One traveled by sea, sailing around the Indian continent and on to the Arabian Peninsula. The northernmost leg passed along the Steppes, north of the Caucus Mountains. The main central route began by paralleling the Great Wall of China, then continuing to the Middle East, traversing deserts and mountain passes. Along that route, there were many famous caravan towns and cities, including Samarkand.

Other trade routes, generally traveling north-and-south, connected the three. One journeyed from the lower Volga region, south along the western shore of the Caspian Sea and through the "iron gate" at the city-fortress of Derbent.

BIBLIOGRAPHY

1. Appleton Company, later called the Encyclopedia Press, Inc; *Catholic Encyclopedia,* 1912,
2. Castor, Helen; *Medieval Times (Births, Marriages, Death),* RLJ Entertainment and Athena Learning.com, Distributed by DCD Rights, Matchlight, BBC Scotland, 2015.
3. Darrah, Marlin; *The Silk Road, The Journey from China to Turkey;* Produced by International Film and Video; distributed by Quester, Inc.; Executive Producer, Albert Nader, 2012.
4. Detres, Raymond and Pieter Plas, *Developing Cultural Identity in the Balkans,* contributing author Nada Alaica, *A Mixing of Cultural Identities, The Croatian Boderlands in the Nineteenth Century,* Presses InterUniversitaires Europeennes, 2005.
5. Farmer, David Hugh; *Margaret of Antioch, The Oxford Dictionary of Saints,* Oxford University Press, 2003.

6. Fine, John V. A., Jr.; *The Early Medieval Balkans: A Critical Survey from the Sixth to the Late Twelfth Century*, The University of Michigan Press, 1983.
7. Finkel, Caroline; *Osman's Dream*, Perseus Books Group, 2005; Mazower, Mark; *The Balkans, A Short History*, Modern Library, an imprint of Random House, 2002.
8. Foley, John Miles; *The Theory of Oral Composition, History and Methodology*, Indiana University Press, 1988.
9. Goodwin, Jason; *Lords of the Horizons*, Henry Hold and Co., 1998.
10. Gordon, Murray; *Slavery in the Arab World*, New Amsterdam Books, 1989.
11. Hain, Kathryn; *Devsirme is a Contested Practice*, Alpha Rho Papers of Phi Alpha Theta, University of Utah, 2012.
12. Jelavi, Barbara; *History of the Balkans, Volume 1. Eighteenth and Nineteenth Centuries*, Cambridge University Press, 1983.
13. Južnič, Dr. Stanislav; *History of Kostel, 1500-1900, Between Two Civilizations*, The Slovenian Genealogy Sociey International, Inc, 2004.
14. Južnič, Dr. Stanislav; *Kostel Under the last Langenmantl*, Historical Newspaper, Vol. Issue 60, 2006.
15. Lewis, Bernard; *Istanbul, and the Civilization of the Ottoman Empire*, University of Oklahoma Press, 1963.
16. Lewis, Bernard; *Race and Slavery in the Middle East: An Historical Enquiry*, Oxford University Press, 1990.
17. Lord, Alfred; *The Singer of Tales*, Lecture by Harvard University Press, 1960.
18. Lord Kinross; *The Ottoman Centuries, the Rise and Fall of the Turkish Empire*, Morrow Quill Paperbacks, 1977.
19. Minkov, Anton; *Kisve, Bahasi, Petitions and Ottoman Social Life 1670-1730*, Vol. 30, Brill, 2004.

20. Murphey, Rhoads; *Ottoman Warfare 1500-1700,* Rutgers University Press, 1999.
21. Nicolson, Adam; *Hay Beautiful,* National Geographic, July 2013.
22. PBS; *Islam, Empire of Faith,* Gardner Films, Inc., 2006.
23. Ryan, William and Walter Pitman; *Noah's Flood,* Simon & Schuster, 1998.
24. St. Erlich, Vera; *Family in Transition, A study of 300 Yugoslav Villages,* Princeton University Press, 1966.
25. Shore, Henry N.; *Signaling Methods Among the Ancients,* United Service Magazine, 1915.
26. Uyar, Mesut and Edward Jerickson; *A Military History of the Ottomans,* Greenwood. Publishing Group, an Imprint of ABC-CLIO, LLC, 2009.
27. Vryonis, Speros, Jr.; *Isidore Glabas and the Turkish Devsirme,* Speculum, A Journal of Medieval Studies, Vol. XXXI, No. 3, Medieval Academy of America, 1956.
28. Westerlind, Eva S; *Carrying the Farm on her Back,* Rainier Books, 1989.

OTHER NOVELS AND SHORT STORIES

By Richard Puz

Novels Six Bulls Series ~

<u>Six Bulls</u>—The Ohioans (print and e-book versions)
Rafting from Ohio to Missouri, down the big rivers of America, pioneers load their families and possessions on flatboats, seeking a new life on the American frontier. Adventures abound during their exciting and dangerous trip.

<u>The Carolinian</u> (print and e-book versions)
Abraham matures during the Battle of New Orleans and later applies those principles on his tobacco plantation in North Carolina. Shunning slavery, he moves his family west. Their adventures produce a riveting account of pioneer life in the wilds of a new country while battling the ever-present Hooker, the slaver.

Avenge **(e-book and print versions)**
The theft of prized horses sets a young man on a journey of adventure. On the trail of the last outlaw, he roams the vast and wild American frontier, tracking a murdering rapist, as the two men clash in an epic battle of wits, in which only one can survive.

Bride by Mail **(e-book and print versions)**
Eva, a strong-willed spinster librarian in Ohio, begins corresponding with Frank, an adventurer living in the wilds of Washington Territory. He regales her about his trip west, traveling with a wagon train—encountering bandits, mining for gold and running cattle. Affection between the two grows, until ...

Short Stories ~

My novels are the basis for these short stories.

Abraham
Abraham, a raw young recruit, experiences the terror of war during the Battle of New Orleans. A frontiersman provides the wisdom to help him become a hero.

Arkansas Storm & Captain Jonathan Buzzard
A steamboat tows pioneers on flatboats on the Arkansas River until the party runs into a storm that threatens their lives and the loss of all they own. In the second story, the big, brawny captain takes on the outlaws threatening his neighbors.

Beanblossom Creek & Stain
Chief Black Hawk's men are on the warpath, and the militia captain and his men are waiting. The battle that follows is tragic and larger-than-life. The second tale finds white settlers conflicted over the brutal treatment of Indians.

Canyon of Death
The greatest killer on the Oregon Trail in the 1800s was unexpected, silent and lethal. This pioneering party comes across a large herd of cattle and drovers who are dying. Read the story about *the* greatest killer on the California and Oregon trails.

Danny Boy and Tennie
Whimsical and humorous—a riverbank tavern on the Ohio River is the setting for pioneers quenching their thirst after a long wagon train journey to Indiana. It is a roaring good time, until a fight breaks out, enlivening the evening. The second story is about Jonah and the green-eyed gal, Tennie, confronting a violent tornado storm.

Newtonia
Settlers on the frontier find themselves between warring armies, as the Civil War rages. In the midst, there is human compassion.

Roaring River
Bushwhackers ambush two men, killing one. The survivor leads a posse in tracking down the band of killers, resulting in the battle of Roaring River.

Runaway Slave
A tobacco plantation owner confronts a split-second decision, which will affect the remainder of his life.

Smoke
Prairies among God's greatest gifts, but they can also be deadly. Rural pioneers take desperate measures, in an attempt to save everything they have created on the wild frontier.

Sourdough Wind Mine
Deep in the bowels of a gold mine, the law enforcer confronts men stealing gold.

Three Bells
Settlers on remote farms in Indiana prepare to defend themselves against Chief Blackhawk and his warriors. One fateful night, an encounter changes everyone forever.

K SERIES OF NOVELS

There are three novels planned for this series. The next one is entitled *White Gold*, scheduled for release in 2017. It begins with the Kostel leasehold by Baron Johan Michael Androcha at the end of the storyteller's recitation in *Blood Tax*. Here is a sample of *White Gold* ~

CHAPTER ONE

Saint George's Day
Market Kostel
1694

On the grassy knoll, Johannes Stefanich, the traveling teller of tales, finished in his singsong voice, strumming the two-string gusle one last time—

> I heard long ago
> And tell in this way
> For you to know

Johannes slowly stood and bowed to the crowd.

People clapped, cheered and shouted with joy, to thank him, the favorite storyteller in the Kupa River Valley. The large crowd rose, excitedly talking about the narrator's performance. Then, yet another rousing round of applause started and again they saluted Stefanich. Many rose and pressed closer, some warily and fearful, others mesmerized by the penetrating look from his hypnotic blue eyes.

A page from the Count, dressed in a forest-green jacket and leggings, pushed through the gathering and managed to reach the storyteller's side. The young man whispered in the storyteller's ear while dropping a purse of coins into the deep pocket of the old man's tunic.

Johannes stopped and stared sharply, first at the page, then at the low rise where the noblemen were seated. Raising his shoulders and eyebrows, he questioned the page's message. A wave of Count Lamberg's hand answered the silent question. Stefanich drew himself up to his full height and raised his hands to quiet the crowd. "Friends, Kostelians, good people of Kostel—please grant me another moment." Repeating his plea, he stood with hands raised, until a semblance of calm had returned. Then, in his booming voice, he announced, "Count Lamberg has requested that he be allowed to address you at this time." Sitting down on the grass again, he watched, curious but also uneasy, as the crowd found places to sit on the ground again.

From his crimson padded chair, the young Count stood and smiled at his serfs. "This will not take long," he began. "It has been a glorious day, and I wish to thank our storyteller for a remarkable poem. Let us give him another round of applause and hope that he will return soon." The crowd complied with loud shouts of "more!"

Finally calming the gathering again, the Count continued, "My dear friends and family. I recently received news from Vienna that I would share with you today. I find that I will be taking another post on behalf of the House of Hapsburg. You know that I already own and manage four fiefdoms and, while I grew up here in Kostel, I must give up some duties to do Vienna's bidding.

"Therefore, I have sold the fiefdom of Kostel to the monarchy and they, in turn, have leased it to the man seated beside me. Beginning next month, I will depart. Baron Johan Michael Androcha and his family will become the new leaseholder, and he will become the Lord of the Castle. I am sure you will be as devoted to him as you have been to me. By way of greeting, the Baron would like to say a few words."

Baron Androcha stood, dressed in a beautiful gold-colored tunic, trimmed in black mink. The man was physically small, with dark hair that was square-cut across the brow. The cut of his shoulder-length hair was the same. He did not smile as his dark, brooding eyes scanned the crowd.

Johannes sensed uneasiness rippling through the people sitting on the ground.

The Baron's unflattering image presented a short, no-nonsense man in his thirties or early forties. A footman hurried toward him, bringing a footstool from the carriage, so that the new Lord was more visible to the assembled gathering, while standing on the stool.

Johannes noticed a crest on the chest of the baron's tunic, which undoubtedly was his family's coat-of-arms. In the center was a vault, representing the heavens arising from the palm of a man's hand. At the top, a halo wrapped the image, set against a blue sky and highlighted with stars of gold.

"Kostelians," the Baron began, in a deep nasal voice, "the most Holy Emperor, through the Council in Vienna, has granted me the leasehold here in Kostel. And, like all owners, the emperor seeks to improve the revenues generated by his lands. All of us know where improvements can begin from this day forward as the storyteller has already relayed Helena's instructions to her family of laying aside a few coins from the tolls."

The man's attempt at humor fell flat, and his broad smile did little to soften his words.

"But that was a century back," he continued, "and I am quite confident the practice of stealing from the Lord of this fiefdom and the Emperor ceased many years ago. Otherwise, it would be very unfortunate for all involved." Again, an awkward smile split the Baron's stern expression.

Still, no one laughed; rather Stanislaus felt the tenseness in the crowd increase. There was no mistaking the baron's threat and its ugly undercurrent. Johannes' blue eyes blazed with fury. He made a small sign of the cross and whispered softly to himself, "*Drek*," shit, he said. "He uses my words against the people he will govern!"

"I have three announcements for today, my new neighbors," the Baron continued. "First, starting in two months, all future taxes will be paid in kind from all the productive activities in Kostel, including berries plucked and firewood cut from the royal forest. There will be no exceptions. Let me repeat, no exceptions. When you grow a bushel of wheat, a portion of that bushel represents the tax, payable in wheat. The same goes for yarn, linen, other crops, wine and livestock. In other words, taxes apply to anything and everything that is grown, made or serviced in this fiefdom. As already noted, no exceptions will be permitted."

The Bishop half-rose from his chair, likely to challenge the mention of no exceptions, as applied to church lands, but Count Lamberg motioned for him to sit down.

A deathly silence came over the crowd, as serfs tried to make sense of the announcement. Most seemed stunned. Until then, they sold their goods anywhere in the empire, then paid taxes in kind or silver coin.

An impudent serf shouted from the safety of the crowd, "What is the reason for this change?"

"An excellent question from a man hiding among the crowd," the Baron answered in a cold manner that did nothing to enhance his image with his new serfs. Continuing, he said, "Vienna has become concerned that bartering between serfs is canceling out many transactions, which then avoid the payment of taxes. Let me give you one simple example. When the blacksmith sharpens the blade of your scythe today, you might repay him by cutting his grass or milking his cow. With that exchange of labor, there is no tax under present rules. The changes I speak of will impose taxes for performing services, such as these. Any tax, of course, is on top of the days of labor that you donate to tending castle lands and fulfilling other duties that I assign on behalf of the castle, the fief and for the greater good of everyone in Kostel. There is no change in that."

The stunned silence continued, as the serfs continued to ponder the changes and wondered how it would affect them and their families.

"Secondly," the Baron continued, "I want to introduce all of you today to Adelmar Lothar von Spear."

A tall and slender, gray-bearded man rose, clothed as a well-dressed soldier. He raised his hand, acknowledging the gathering and then sat again. His eyes had a glint, as he shrewdly surveyed the crowd, stroking his beard.

"He becomes the new Captain of the Guard at the castle and my chief tax collector for Kostel. I know that everyone will have an opportunity to meet him, along with his men, as they will be traveling from village to village and visiting every hide."

The crowd's shock could not have been greater, for many had heard about von Spear and stories about his heavy-handed ways in other fiefdoms from passing travelers.

The new Castle Lord continued, "And, I close with this last announcement. Under my leasehold, the tax you have been paying on imported salt will double."

Involuntarily, a shout of "no" rose from the crowd. Kostel was self-sufficient in everything except one thing upon which the lives of every person and animal depended on—salt! Because of the critical necessity, many called it "white gold."

Terrible difficulties lay ahead, and Johannes felt a shudder of disbelief run through the gathering, all of whom were now standing. Angry murmurs gave way to soft cursing and fuming under-the-breath outbursts.

These drifted to his ears. Slowly, he made his way through the gathering, two-string-<u>gusle</u> in one hand and seat cushion in the other. *It might be a long time before I return to Kostel*, he speculated. *Trouble is brewing here— maybe even rebellion.*

Katarina Klobucar made her way through the crowd with her husband, Andreas, and their children. "How will these changes affect our lives?" she asked, looking at him. "It sounds bad to me."

"I am unsure about paying taxes in kind," her husband responded. "But, I know that doubling the tax on salt from two dinars to four is trouble for everyone. We usually sell farm goods, such as wine or hemp, to obtain coins to buy our salt. Without our being able to earn coins, how do we pay the increased tax on salt . . . ?"

www.ingramcontent.com/pod-product-compliance
Lightning Source LLC
Chambersburg PA
CBHW060148050426
42446CB00013B/2726